MW01267593

GREAT
MILITARY LEADERS
of the 20TH Century

DOUGLAS MACARTHUR
MAO ZEDONG
GEORGE S. PATTON
JOHN J. PERSHING
ERWIN J.E. ROMMEL
H. NORMAN SCHWARZKOPF

GREAT
MILITARY LEADERS
of the 20TH Century

GEORGE S. PATTON

EARLE RICE JR.

INTRODUCTION BY
CASPAR W. WEINBERGER

SERIES CONSULTING EDITOR
EARLE RICE JR.

CHELSEA HOUSE
PUBLISHERS
A Haights Cross Communications Company
Philadelphia

FRONTIS: **Patton on the train station platform at Toul, France, in October 1944.**

CHELSEA HOUSE PUBLISHERS
VP, NEW PRODUCT DEVELOPMENT Sally Cheney
DIRECTOR OF PRODUCTION Kim Shinners
CREATIVE MANAGER Takeshi Takahashi
MANUFACTURING MANAGER Diann Grasse

STAFF FOR GEORGE S. PATTON
EXECUTIVE EDITOR Lee Marcott
PRODUCTION ASSISTANT Megan Emery
PICTURE RESEARCHER Sarah Bloom
SERIES & COVER DESIGNER Keith Trego
LAYOUT 21st Century Publishing and Communications, Inc.

A Haights Cross Communications ✈ Company

http://www.chelseahouse.com

First Printing

1 3 5 7 9 8 6 4 2

Library of Congress Cataloging-in-Publication Data applied for.

ISBN 0-7910-7403-X

TABLE OF CONTENTS

INTRODUCTION

by Caspar W. Weinberger

At a time when it is ever more apparent that the world will need skilled and bold military leaders, it is both appropriate and necessary that school history courses include studies of great military leaders.

Democracies, for the most part, are basically not greatly interested in military leadership or military matters in general. Fortunately, in the United States we have sufficient interest and volunteers for military service so that we can maintain and staff a very strong military with volunteers— people who want to serve.

That is very fortunate indeed for us. Volunteers and those who decide of their own free will that they want to be in the military are, generally speaking, easier to train, and to retain in the services, and their morale is markedly higher than that of conscripts. Furthermore, the total effect of a draft, based on our Vietnam experience, can be very bad— indeed it can polarize the country as a whole.

One of the best ways of ensuring that we will continue to have enough volunteers in the future is to study the great accomplishments of our past military leaders—the small group of leaders and others who contributed so much to our past greatness and our present strength.

Not all of these leaders have been Americans, but the

example that all of them set are well worth studying in our schools. Of the six military leaders chosen by Chelsea House's "Great Military Leaders of the 20th Century," I had the privilege of serving under and with two.

In World War II, after two years of volunteer service in the infantry at home and in the Pacific, I was transferred from the 41st infantry division then in New Guinea, to General Douglas MacArthur's intelligence staff in Manila, in the Philippines. One of my assignments was to prepare drafts of the general's daily communiqué to other theater commanders around the world. This required seeing all of the major military cable and intelligence information, and digesting the most important items for his daily report to the other war theaters of the world. It also required a familiarity with our plans to carry the war to the enemy as soon as sufficient strength had been transferred to our theater from Europe.

The invasion of Japan toward which all the planning was aiming would have been a very difficult and costly operation. Most of the tentative plans called for landing our force on one of the southern Japanese islands, and another force on Honshu, north of Tokyo.

We know that Japan's troops would have fought fiercely and very skillfully once their homeland was invaded. In fact, all of our plans forecast that we would lose virtually all of the first two U.S. divisions that landed. That was one of the main reasons that President Harry Truman concluded we had to use the atomic bomb. That ended the war, and all landings taken in Japan were peaceful and unopposed.

Many years later, when I was secretary of defense under President Ronald Reagan, a part of my duties was to recommend generals and admirals for various U.S. and NATO regional commands. Fulfilling this duty led me to interview several possible candidates for the post of commander in chief of our Central Command, which had jurisdiction over our many military activities in the Middle East.

My strong recommendation, accepted by the president, was that he name General H. Norman Schwarzkopf to lead the Central Command. A short time later, General Schwarzkopf led our forces in that region to the great military victory of the Gulf War.

General MacArthur and General Schwarzkopf shared many of the same qualities. Both were very experienced army officers tested by many widely different conditions all over the world. Both were calm, resolute, and inspirational leaders. Both were superb military planners and developers of complex and very large-scale military operations. Both achieved great military successes; both had the best interest of all our troops at heart; and both were leaders in the best sense of the word. They both had the ability and skills necessary to work with military and civilian leaders of our allies and friends in all parts of the globe.

It is vitally important for our future as a democracy, a superpower and a country whose strengths have helped save freedom and peace, that our children and our schools know far more about these leaders and countless others like them who serve the cause of peace with freedom so well and so faithfully. Their lives and the lives of others like them will be a great inspiration for us and for later generations who need to know what America at its best can accomplish.

The other military leaders whose lives are presented in this series include a German, General Erwin Rommel, and the former Communist China leader, Mao Zedong.

General Rommel won many preliminary battles in the desert war of World War II before losing the decisive battle of El Alamein. He had to develop and execute his tactics for desert fighting under conditions not previously experienced by him or his troops. He also became one of the masters of the art of tank warfare.

Mao Zedong had to train, develop, arm, and deploy huge numbers of Chinese soldiers to defeat the organized and experienced forces of Chiang Kai-shek's Nationalist government. He accomplished this and, in comparatively short time, won the military victories that transformed his country.

Both of these generals had to learn, very quickly, the new tactics needed to cope with rapidly changing conditions. In short, they had to be flexible, inventive, and willing and able to fight against larger opposing forces and in unfamiliar environments.

This whole series demonstrates that great military success requires many of the qualities and skills required for success in other fields of endeavor. Military history is indeed a vital part of the whole story of mankind, and one of the best ways of studying that history is to study the lives of those who succeeded by their leadership in this vital field.

CASPAR W. WEINBERGER
CHAIRMAN, *FORBES* INC
MARCH 2003

CASPAR W. WEINBERGER was the fifteenth U.S. secretary of defense, serving under President Ronald Reagan from 1981 to 1987, longer than any previous defense secretary except Robert McNamara (served 1961–1968). Weinberger is also an author who has written books about his experiences in the Reagan administration and about U.S. military capabilities.

"Hero of the Tanks"

On September 26, 1918, Lieutenant Colonel George S. Patton Jr. abandoned the ranks of ordinary battlefield commanders and joined the select fraternity of great warrior leaders. He enrolled in the premier brotherhood on the first day of the Meuse-Argonne offensive. The offensive lasted for 47 days and resulted in Germany's surrender and the end of World War I. His role as commander of the U.S. First Tank Brigade in the Allied drive lasted only a few hours. But a few hours were all that he needed to conquer fear and establish himself as an extraordinary officer and leader of men.

In the early autumn of 1918, the grand design of the Allies—principally England, France, and the United States—called

Patton's road to fame as a military leader began in France during World War I. As Lieutenant Colonel and tank corps commander, Patton led a successful advance against entrenched German positions despite poor weather, supply problems, and a gunshot wound to the thigh. Afterward, he was promoted to full colonel and hailed as the "Hero of the Tanks."

for a series of offensives across the entire Western Front. French Marshal Ferdinand Foch, supreme commander of Allied forces in Europe, established September 26 as D day, the day when the first offensive would begin. He assigned the task of initiating attacks in the Meuse-Argonne to General John J. "Black Jack" Pershing's U.S. First Army and General Henri J. E. Gouraud's French Fourth Army. Massive Allied attacks by British, Belgian, French, Australian, and American forces were slated to follow in the days ahead, all aimed at crushing the German Hindenburg Line.

Pershing's First Army had just successfully completed the reduction of the St.-Mihiel salient, a forward bulge in the German lines, on September 16. With D day for the new offensive only ten days away, Pershing faced the awesome task of moving more than a million men with tanks and guns (cannon) 60 miles northwest of St.-Mihiel over an inadequate road and rail network during the rainy season. He assigned the job to Colonel George C. Marshall, the First Army G-3 (operations officer) and a future chief of staff of the army. Marshall's carefully laid plans quickly proved unworkable. He later wrote:

> They broke down almost from the beginning. Thousands of the 90,000 horses that were hauling supplies through the waterlogged country near the Meuse [river] collapsed or died in their tracks, causing monumental traffic jams. In the almost constant drizzle, engineers worked tirelessly with rocks and gravel, mud and logs to repair mired roads.[1]

But every night, men sweated and toiled on the roads in the mud and incessant rains and somehow got the job done. Infantryman Private Rush S. Young of the Eightieth Division summed up the enormous shift of men and matériel: "Everyone and everything was trying to get along at the same time."[2]

Patton's tanks and tankers (tank soldiers) fared a little better. They returned to the railhead at St.-Mihiel and entrained on flat cars for the journey. The brigade later offloaded in the rain and at the dead of night at the rail siding at Clermont-en-Argonne. Under the circumstances, the swift relocation of a tank brigade represented a hazardous, near-impossible task. Patton accomplished the movement with fair success but not without his share of problems. "One fine example of efficiency nix [negation] just happened," he wrote later in a letter to his much-adored wife Beatrice. "100,000 gallons of gas arrived in tank cars with no pump. Now we can't get it out except by dippers!!!"[3] Despite a number of mishaps that such a move entails, Patton somehow managed to complete the move and position his brigade for attack in a timely way.

General Pershing's plan called for the First Army to attack from the south across a 24-mile front that stretched from the Argonne Forest to the Meuse River. On the American left flank, General Gouraud's Fourth Army would launch its offensive to the west. Pershing spanned the 24-mile front with three corps. He assigned Patton's tank brigade to support two National Guard divisions of Major General Hunter Liggett's I Corps—the Twenty-Eighth from Pennsylvania, and the Thirty-Fifth from Kansas-Missouri.

The Twenty-Eighth was to advance north along the eastern edge of the Argonne Forest, while the Thirty-Fifth attacked across the open ground north of the Vauquois Heights. Patton personally scouted the entire area and found only a narrow strip along the right flank of the Twenty-Eighth Division suitable for tank operations. Further complicating the battlefield situation, the Aire River flowed between the two American divisions and parallel to their axis of advance, removing the possibility of mutual support.

In a memorandum, Patton described the terrain as "an old battle-ground, heavily seamed with trenches and pitted with numerous shell-holes."[4] Despite the unfavorable ground, he pledged to dispose his tanks in such a way as to offer the best chance for success, even though their deployment might not be considered "in accordance with most preconceived notions as to the proper use of tanks."[5]

Patton's First Tank Brigade consisted of the 344th Tank Battalion commanded by Major Sereno Brett, and the

345th Tank Battalion under Captain Ranulf Compton. Each battalion was divided into three companies. The brigade was reinforced by the French Fourteenth and Seventeenth Groupes led by Major C.M.M. Chanoine. Patton's tankers were equipped with French-built Renault light tanks, whereas Chanoine's groups were outfitted with heavier Schneider tanks. All told, Patton would enter the battle with about 140 tanks.

The terrain facing the Americans in the Meuse-Argonne heavily favored the German defenders. Over the past four years, they had established three defensive belts in front of their fourth—and main—entrench-ment, known to the Allies as the Hindenburg Line (but to the Germans as the Siegfried Line). A fifth defensive belt, called the Freya *Stellung* (emplacement), backed up the main line. The labyrinth of German fortifications extended 12 miles deep. Interlocking bands of machine-gun fire from nests set in concrete and protected by barbed wire dominated the American sector from the heights of Montfaucon, Cunel, Romagne, and Barricourt.

Describing the sector later, Brigadier General Hugh A. Drum, First Army chief of staff, stated: "This was the most ideal defensive terrain I have ever seen or read about."[6] Only the fact that just five German divisions defended the 24-mile front favored the Americans. But Pershing knew that the Germans had the ability to reinforce the sector rapidly with another 15 divisions.

The American commander planned to surprise and overwhelm the Germans with massive force, thrusting through the outer defenses to the Hindenburg Line within 24 hours. He would thus prevent German reinforcements from moving forward. To this end, 250,000 American assault troops moved into position along the 24-mile front in the predawn hours of September 26, 1918.

During World War I, Patton's leadership helped prove that the tank was a formidable military tool. In France's Argonne Forest, American tanks made critical advances against German positions. Patton was able to conquer his fears, inspire his men, and make bold strikes against enemy positions.

In the I Corps sector, because of the terrain limitations, Patton decided to use one of Major Brett's tank companies of the 344th Tank Battalion in the narrow corridor bordering the Argonne Forest on the Twenty-Eighth Division's right flank. Across the Aire River, in the open terrain better suited to tank operations, he deployed Brett's other two tank companies behind the Thirty-Fifth Division. Patton held Captain Compton's less-experienced tank battalion and Major Chanoine's two groups in reserve. After Brett's tankers secured the first objective, the reserves were to move through Brett's battalion in column and seize the next two objectives. On the eve of battle, Patton wrote to Beatrice:

> Just a word to you before I leave to play a little part in what promises to be the biggest battle of the war or world so far. . . .
>
>   I am always nearvous [sic] about this time just as at Polo or Foot ball before the game starts but so far I have been all right after that. I hope I keep on that way.[7]

At 2:30 A.M. on September 26, Allied artillery opened fire with a preparatory barrage that rocked the foundations of Europe. According to one American corps commander, the bombardment sounded like "the collision of a million express trains."[8] During the next three hours, the big guns hammered the lines of German army commander General Max von Gallwitz with more ammunition than both sides had expended during the entire four years of the American Civil War. The cost of the thunderous barrage was later calculated at $180 million—or a million dollars a minute.

At 5:30 A.M., which had been designated as H hour—the preset time to start the offensive—the Americans began their advance in a heavy mist. A rolling artillery barrage replaced the preparatory bombardment and began chewing up the ground—as well as any hapless Germans—just in front of them. Some of Brett's leading tanks soon ran into a mine field, but as Patton noted later, "thanks to the courtesy of the Germans in leaving up warning signs [ACHTUNG MINEN, or ATTENTION MINES] the tanks avoided this danger."[9]

Brett's tanks moved ahead smartly under the covering mists that not only veiled their progress from the Germans but also from Patton's observation in his command post (CP), a crude dugout in a woods outside Neuvilly. Two weeks earlier, during the fighting at St.-Mihiel, Patton had left his command post to join the forward action. For leaving his CP, he had received a strong rebuke from Colonel Samuel D. Rockenbach, commander of the American Expeditionary Force (AEF) Tank Corps. He did not need another reprimand. By 6:30 A.M., however, hearing the sounds of battle ahead but unable to see a thing through the dense mists, he could not contain himself any longer. With two officers, a half-dozen runners, and a few carrier pigeons, he walked toward the sound of the guns.

Following in the tracks of his tanks, Patton and his little group moved toward the village of Cheppy, passing some French tanks and later Compton's tanks. "It was terribly foggy and in addition they [American artillery] were shooting smoke shells so we could not see ten feet," Patton wrote later. "Machine guns were going in every direction in front, behind, and on both sides."[10] In the fog, they could not tell whether the fire was American, German, or both as they plodded slowly forward.

The fog lifted about 10:00 A.M. By then, Patton's small troop had drawn to within 500 yards of Cheppy — and, to everyone's surprise, to a position some 250 yards ahead of Compton's reserve tanks. With the improved visibility, they suddenly became targets for incoming artillery and machine-gun fire. Patton ordered them to take cover in a nearby railway cut. Scribbling out a message to inform Colonel Rockenbach of his relocation, he sent it off by carrier pigeon and settled back to await the arrival of Compton's tanks.

While Patton waited for Compton to bring his tanks forward, several groups of panicking soldiers who had become separated from their units came running to the rear. He stopped them and herded them into the railway cut. Before he knew it, he had collected about 100 of them. When the German gunners began to find the range of the railway cut, their fire became much more intensive. Patton led his own group and the stragglers to a small hill about 100 yards to the rear and fanned them out on its reverse slope. From his new vantage point, he noticed several of Compton's tanks about another 125 yards to the rear, at the base of the hill.

Patton sent one of his officers to investigate why the tanks had not come forward and learned that the tanks had become bogged down in two enormous trenches that the Germans had held until recently. French tankers were trying to dig away the banks of the trenches, but when German shells and bullets started flying in their direction, they tossed their shovels aside and just sat in the trenches for protection.

After sending several of his men down the hill in unsuccessful efforts to spur the tankers into moving forward, Patton — now growing angrier by the minute — ran down the hill himself. When Patton saw the Frenchmen just sitting in the trenches, he adjusted their attitudes in an instant. First Lieutenant Paul S. Edwards, Patton's signal officer, described what happened next. Under heavy machine-gun and artillery fire, Patton immediately:

> . . . went over to the tanks which were being splattered with machine gun fire and removed the shovels and picks and put the men to work. . . . In spite of repeated requests that he step down in the trench from his exposed position the Colonel steadfastly refused to do so saying, "To Hell with them — they can't hit me.[11]

When they at last moved five tanks across the trench, Patton sent them on up the hill. Then, waving high the large walking stick that he carried to tap on tanks as a means of communicating with them, he shouted, "Let's go get them. Who is with me?"[12] and he strode off up the hill.

The Argonne was a costly yet decisive battle both for Allied forces and for Patton himself. Despite a hail of German machine-gun fire, Patton led his tanks through rough terrain. Though injured by a German bullet, Patton continued to direct his troops, showing grit and determination in the face of obvious danger.

At the crest of the hill, a rain of steel from German machine guns greeted Patton and his followers, and they flung themselves to the ground. At that moment, Patton "felt a great desire to run."[13] But he then experienced a strange battlefield vision:

> I was trembling with fear when suddenly I thought of my progenitors [ancestors] and seemed to see them in a cloud over the German lines looking at me. I became calm at once and saying aloud "It is time for another Patton to die," called for volunteers and went forward to what I honestly believed to be certain death.[14]

Again waving his stick high above his head, Patton shouted, "Let's go, let's go!"[15] and started forward. Six men followed him. Five went down, dead.

Private First Class Joseph T. Angelo, Patton's orderly, said, "We are alone."[16]

Patton replied, "Come on anyway,"[17] and an unknown something drove him forward again. Seconds later, a machine-gun bullet ripped into his left upper thigh and exited through his left buttock, leaving a hole the size of a silver dollar. He lapsed into shock immediately but somehow managed to remain conscious. Angelo helped him to "a small shell hole,"[18] where he stopped Patton's bleeding and bandaged his wound.

Several tanks appeared soon afterward. Using his orderly as his legs, he sent Angelo to point out the German machine guns to them. (The Americans later determined that there were at least 25 machine-gun nests defending Cheppy, a vital first-day objective.) When a sergeant came by, Patton told him to spread the word about his wound and to find Brett and inform him that he was now in command of the First Tank Brigade. Refusing to be evacuated, he continued—through Angelo—to direct advancing tanks to their targets. His tankers moved forward and captured Varennes and Cheppy, then paused in front of Montfaucon to allow the infantry time to catch up with them before continuing their assault.

That afternoon, after the fighting had left Patton far behind, three stretcher bearers came for him and—at his insistence—carried him back to division headquarters. Patton gave a full battle report of the morning's action to a divisional officer. Only afterward did he allow himself to be driven to an evacuation hospital.

When he awoke the next morning, he found two of his tank officers in beds next to his own. Newspaper stories were already lionizing him as the "Hero of the Tanks"[19] for continuing to direct his tanks from a shell hole in spite of the severity of his wound. For his singular effort in the Meuse-Argonne, Patton received a promotion to full colonel and the Distinguished Service Cross, the army's second-highest award for valor in combat.

In a single morning, Patton had accomplished two things of lasting importance: He had demonstrated to friend and foe alike that the tank was a force to be reckoned with in modern warfare, and he had proved to himself that he was not a coward. In a subsequent letter to his father, the "Hero of the Tanks" wrote, "I have always feared I was a coward at heart but I am beginning to doubt it."[20] The warrior was coming of age.

2

Another Soldier in the Family

Born in San Gabriel, California, on November 11, 1885, George Smith Patton Jr. descended from a Virginia family with a long and distinguished military tradition. The Patton roots in America trace back to the eighteenth century to a Scottish immigrant of unknown ancestry who arrived in Virginia and took the name of Robert Patton. In 1771, Robert acquired a deed of land in Fredericksburg. He prospered over the next 20 years and rose sufficiently in the finest circles of Virginia society to enable his marriage to Anne Gordon Mercer.

Anne was the daughter of Hugh Mercer, an esteemed physician who had also emigrated from Scotland. Hugh, a close friend of George Washington, rose to the rank of brigadier general in the

Continental Army and died a hero's death at Princeton in the Revolutionary War. Young George adopted his revolutionary forebear as a role model and took to heart the Mercer family creed that Hugh had exemplified: "Then, Mercer, bear ye bravely, do no shame. Nor blot the scutcheon [a shield or emblem bearing a coat of arms] of our ancient name."[21]

Robert and Anne Patton had seven children, including John Mercer Patton, born in 1797. John became a lawyer and a governor of Virginia. He wedded Margaret French Williams, descended from the Slaughters of Culpeper County. They produced 12 offspring. Seven of their sons— among them George's paternal grandfather, the first to bear the George Smith Patton name—distinguished themselves in the Civil War on the Confederate side.

Three of the Patton brothers studied under Thomas J. Jackson—later known as "Stonewall"—and graduated from the Virginia Military Institute (VMI). The Patton brothers fought in the Mississippi Valley and at Gettysburg, Second Manassas, and Cold Harbor. Young George drew inspiration from his six great-uncles, but he honored most his paternal grandfather and namesake.

The first George Smith Patton graduated from VMI in 1852 and practiced law in Charleston, West Virginia. In 1855, he married Susan Thornton Glassell. Susan's lineage extended back to George Washington's great-grandfather, King Edward I of England, and to King Philip III of France. "Even farther in the dim recesses of time were sixteen barons who signed the Magna Carta," writes Martin Blumenson, one of Patton's biographers, "all of whom the Pattons believed were their direct ancestors."[22] The marriage of George and Susan yielded two daughters and two sons, including the second George Smith Patton.

During the Civil War, George's grandfather served under Jubal Early, a renowned Confederate general. Rising

Patton's military roots stretched back as far as the American Civil War. His grandfather, the first George Smith Patton, graduated from the Virginia Military Institute in 1852 and commanded the 22nd Virginia Infantry Regiment. He died in battle at Winchester, Virginia, in 1864.

to the rank of colonel, he commanded the Twenty-Second Virginia Infantry in the Third Battle of Winchester (September 19, 1864), Early's unsuccessful defense of the upper Shenandoah Valley. Colonel Patton fell mortally wounded at the head of his troops in the battle that cost both sides about 5,000 casualties.

In addition to the foregoing warriors, a number of George's cousins held high rank during the war—one Mercer, three Pattons, and at least three Slaughters.

George did not lack for soldierly icons to emulate. He literally believed that his departed kinsmen looked down from above, eternally protective of their warrior legacies and always ready to praise or condemn the actions of their descendants. George vowed as a boy never to dishonor them. "Men of my blood . . . have ever inspired me,"[23] he wrote. He devoted himself to living up to his military heritage and continually tested himself lest his conduct should prove unworthy of the always-present ghosts of his ancestors. "Should I falter, I will have disgraced my blood."[24]

After the Civil War, Susan Thornton Glassell Patton, George's widowed great-grandmother, left the devastated South and moved to California, where she married George Hugh Smith, a lawyer in her brother's law firm of Glassell and Chapman. Smith, also a VMI graduate, had commanded the Sixty-Second Virginia Infantry as a colonel during the war. His refusal to swear allegiance to the Union at war's end, as was required of ex-Confederate officers, had forced him to migrate westward.

Soon after Susan married again, her son George changed his middle name from William to Smith in honor of his new stepfather. He thus became the second George Smith Patton—the man who was to become "Papa" to the son he would call "the Boy."[25]

The future Papa continued the Patton tradition at VMI. But in 1878, after graduating and tutoring French for a year, he returned to California to read and practice law with the firm of Glassell, Smith, and Chapman. After his election as district attorney of Los Angeles County in 1884 seemed to assure his future, he married Ruth Wilson, the daughter of B.D. Wilson, one of California's founding fathers.

Benjamin Davis Wilson was a larger-than-life character whose history abounded with the stuff of fiction. At various times in his adventurous life, "Don Benito," as he was often called, was a pioneer, beaver trapper and trader, grizzly bear hunter, Indian fighter, justice of the peace, farmer, rancher, politician, horticulturist, real estate entrepreneur, vintner, and one of Southern California's great landholders. Don Benito died in 1878 and did not live to see the birth of his daughter's only son and daughter.

George Smith Patton Jr. was born seven years later in Don Benito's ranch home called Lake Vineyard, which was nestled in the foothills of the San Gabriel Mountains and overlooked a lake by the same name. His sister Anita, called "Nita," came along two years later, after the family had moved to Los Angeles to be closer to the elder Patton's work. Although young George owed much to his mother's side of the family, he never regarded his maternal grandfather with the same esteem that he appeared to reserve for the men in his father's lineage. Yet he exhibited many of Don Benito's characteristics. As biographer Blumenson points out, Don Benito:

> . . . seemed to have transmitted to him his physical hardihood, mental perseverance, personal charisma, and driving willpower. Patton never wished to hear of his resemblance to Wilson, for Wilson was a self-made man and quite unlike the Patton aristocrats. Yet he was a ghost too, and Patton feared him.[26]

Young George suffered from dyslexia, a brain condition that causes an abnormal difficulty in reading and spelling. He was also afflicted with what is known today as attention deficit disorder, a neurological-chemical disorder. Both abnormalities generate feelings of inferiority, a limited concentration span, impaired learning skills, a tendency to become easily frustrated with books and studies, and the need to achieve in other areas to make up for these shortcomings. To spare George any potential ridicule by his classmates over his reading and writing mistakes, Papa hired tutors to help him overcome his difficulties while the family lived in Los Angeles.

Papa often read the classics to George aloud. George especially enjoyed Sir Walter Scott, whose tales of Scottish life and lore, clans and tartans, bagpipes and battles, and a chivalrous age long past strengthened his ties with the Patton heritage. Some of his other preferences included Homer's *Iliad* and *Odyssey*, Xenophon's *Anabasis*, Shakespeare, Kipling, and the Old Testament. Like other late-readers who learn by the spoken word, he often memorized and recited lengthy passages of poetry and prose that held a particularly cogent meaning for him. He would perpetuate his passion for poetry throughout his life.

The boy's Aunt Nannie, Ruth's sister Annie, also read aloud to him. He delighted in such classics as Plutarch's *Lives, The March of Xenophon, Alexander the Great,* and, as George's grandson Robert H. Patton would later write, "anything and everything about Napoleon."[27] Continuing, Robert writes:

> He had Siegfried and Beowulf for his heroes; and Robert E. Lee and Stonewall Jackson. The stories of the Civil War he heard right from the men who fought it . . . Georgie lived and played in the company of heroes, dead and alive."[28]

But the Bible, Robert asserts, towered over George's other favorites: "Nannie's religious reading made her nephew's head swirl with alluring myths and legends that coalesced like a planet from a gaseous cloud into a worldview all his own."[29] With his head filled with epic tales of heroism, it did not take the boy long to decide on a career. He opted to become a soldier at the age of five. Up until then, young George had leaned toward joining the fire brigade.

In 1897, when George was 11 years old, his father sacrificed a political or judicial career to administer the Wilson interests in the San Gabriel Valley, and the family moved back to Lake Vineyard. Even when they had lived in town, the family had spent much of their time at the modest yet spacious ranch house. By then, George, through perseverance and determination, had overcome some of his feelings of inadequacy, but he still had not learned to read, write, or calculate. Papa enrolled him in the Classical School for Boys in nearby Pasadena. George soon learned how to express himself fluently and forcefully on paper, but he never learned how to spell well, and mathematics never came easy to him.

At Pasadena, George, now stocky and athletic, made steady but unspectacular progress. He grew to love history—particularly military history—and started studying the lives of the great leaders of ancient times. His knowledge of the past would later prove an invaluable asset in his military career. "A picture without a background is both uninteresting and misleading," he once wrote. "Hence, in order to paint you an intelligent picture . . . as it exists today, we must provide an historical background."[30]

George's formative years at Lake Vineyard slipped by swiftly. "Papa" Patton taught his son horsemanship, marksmanship, how to hunt, how to dress to perfection—Papa always dressed for dinner—pride in his family heritage, and the importance of good breeding. Papa's teachings would serve the boy well in his future profession. These were George's golden days. As he once put it, "I must be the happiest boy in the world."[31]

In the summer of 1902, just before his last year at the Classical School for Boys, Beatrice Banning Ayer slipped

As a boy, Patton suffered from several learning disorders, probably those known today as dyslexia and attention deficit disorder. His father, the second George Smith Patton, or "Papa," took a great interest in his son's education, hiring private tutors to help his son overcome his disabilities.

into George's life. Beatrice was the cultured daughter of multimillionaire Massachusetts industrialist Frederick Ayer. She and her family spent the summer visiting with their relatives, the Bannings of nearby Wilmington.

The Bannings and the Pattons were good friends. The two families customarily vacationed together on Catalina

Island. That summer, the Ayer family joined them, and George and Beatrice felt instantly attracted to each other. Years later, their daughter Ruth Ellen Patton Totten would write, "By the end of . . . the summer, Ma and Georgie were in love for the rest of their lives."[32] When the summer ended, the two young people went their separate ways, but they stayed in touch by mail. And neither left the thoughts of the other for long until their deaths.

In 1903, George followed his father and grandfather into the Virginia Military Institute, which, with a little additional help from his father, virtually guaranteed his admittance to the U.S. Military Academy at West Point the following year. Papa Patton called upon a number of his political connections to lobby U.S. Senator Thomas R. Bard for his son's appointment to a single opening in the academy's plebe (freshman) class of 1904. At Papa's request, Judge Henry T. Lee, a former Union officer and prominent Los Angeles Republican, tendered this recommendation for George: "He is a well bred and a well brought up young fellow . . . [who] has developed a great taste and aptitude for the study of military history and the sciences. . . . If blood counts for anything, he certainly comes of fighting stock."[33] The senator received a flood of similar recommendations, and young George entered West Point in June 1904.

Upon entering the academy, George—hereafter called Patton or GSP—vowed to himself to achieve the rank of Class Adjutant, the highest rank a cadet could hold. The rank was usually conferred upon a handsome cadet who dresses to perfection and most exemplifies soldierly conduct, while demonstrating the ability to command and instill discipline. GSP held no illusions as to what lay ahead, acknowledging to his father that West Point would be "the Hell to come."[34] Life in the academy's Corps of Cadets gave him no reason to change his mind.

Patton's years at the U.S. Military Academy gave little hint of the greatness that was to follow. After scoring low grades, he was forced to repeat his freshman year, and at the time of his graduation he finished in the middle of his class. Yet, young Patton had already begun to develop the athletic skills and determination that would serve him later in life. Here we see the young Patton as a cadet at VMI in 1903.

West Point

The U.S. Military Academy at West Point, New York – "West Point" – was founded on March 16, 1802, originally as a school for engineers. Located 50 miles north of New York City, the academy stands on 16,000 acres of high ground overlooking the Hudson River.

The academy opened on July 4, 1802, but at first suffered from organizational and disciplinary problems. On April 29, 1812, an act of Congress reorganized the academy, increased its enrollment to 250 cadets, expanded its staff, and instituted a four-year curriculum. But the goal of the legislators went unrealized until the appointment of Colonel Sylvanus Thayer as superintendent. During his tenure (1817–1833), he became known as the "father of the military academy" because of his enduring influence on its physical properties, library, curriculum, and teaching methods. Under Thayer's direction, the academy produced finely trained graduates whose skills provided the essential civil-engineering services to a nation bent on internal improvement and westward expansion.

Another act of Congress on April 29, 1866, authorized the selection of academy superintendents from branches of the army other than solely the Corps of Engineers. The academy came under the direct control of the Department of the Army, whose authority is vested in the superintendent and who commands both the academy and the military post.

The rigorous West Point curriculum now offers a four-year college-level education leading to a Bachelor of Science degree and a commission of second lieutenant in the U.S. Army. The balanced study course, now open to 4,417 cadets, covers mathematics and basic and engineering sciences, military science, the humanities and social science, and physical education. A cadet candidate must be at least 17 and not yet 22 years old, must be unmarried at the time of appointment, must have a high-school education or its equivalent, and must take a scholastic-aptitude test and a medical examination before admission.

Besides George S. Patton Jr., other illustrious graduates of the academy include Ulysses S. Grant, William T. Sherman, Robert E. Lee, Thomas J. "Stonewall" Jackson, John J. Pershing, Douglas MacArthur, Omar N. Bradley, Dwight D. Eisenhower, and H. Norman Schwarzkopf.

Patton did not come up to the academy's high standards in his first year. Rather than being discharged, however, he was turned back and forced to repeat the year. The extra year showed him to be a "late bloomer" and afforded him the time that he needed to fully mature. During the next four years, he immersed himself mentally in the academy's rigorous curriculum leading to a Bachelor of Science degree, yet he still found time to excel in individual sports: swimming, riding, pistol shooting, cross-country running, and track events. Over the entire five years at West Point, GSP continued to correspond—and to occasionally meet—with Beatrice Banning Ayer.

Five tough years ended for Patton on June 11, 1909, when he graduated as Class Adjutant and received his commission as second lieutenant in the U.S. Army. Patton finished 46th in his class, about in the middle. It was not an outstanding ranking, but neither was it a poor one for a student hampered by dyslexia. He now stood prepared to start his long climb to the lofty heights of high command—for George Smith Patton Jr. had no intention of settling for becoming just another soldier in the family.

Vanguard
of a New Era

Before pinning on the bright gold bars of a second lieutenant, Patton agonized over what branch of the army to apply for, based on which one would afford him the best opportunities for rapid advancement to high command. On the advice of Captain Charles P. Summerall, a regular army officer on the West Point faculty and a good friend and future mentor, Patton chose the cavalry. His choice marked the first important milestone in his military career. He received orders to report in September to K Troop at Fort Sheridan, Illinois. K Troop formed a part of the Fifteenth Cavalry Regiment that was also based at Fort Myer, Virginia, and Fort Leavenworth, Kansas.

Patton spent most of the summer of 1909 fishing off Catalina

During the summer of 1902, before his final year at the Classical School for Boys, Patton met the woman who would later become his wife—Beatrice Banning Ayer, the daughter of a Massachusetts millionaire. Patton and Beatrice wed on May 26, 1910.

Island. He also spent a very pleasant week visiting with Beatrice and her family on Boston's North Shore—sailing, dancing, and partying. He found it easy to like the good life that enormous wealth sustains and was unprepared for the stark contrast of army life at Fort Sheridan.

Although his quarters at West Point had been scarcely more than adequate, they seemed lavish in comparison to the slum-like living conditions of an underfunded peace-time army. In a letter to Beatrice, he described his living accommodations—two rooms on the third floor of the bachelor officers' quarters—as "pretty bad . . . empty and very dirty. Save for one mahoginy desk . . . and an iron bed there is no furniture." [35] Fort Sheridan was a far cry from the "good life" of Boston's North Shore. But it was the life he had chosen, and he planned to make something good come of his first assignment.

Two things are vital to a young career officer: gaining the confidence and trust of his superiors, and earning the respect of his subordinates. At Fort Sheridan, he achieved both in short order. Almost overnight, K Troop commander Captain Francis C. Marshall characterized him as "a young officer of especial promise." [36] And when injured in an incident involving an unruly horse, GSP earned a reputation for "guts" with his men when he continued to drill impassively with his squad for another 20 minutes, all the while bleeding like a "stuck pig." [37]

Once embarked on his army career, he began thinking of marriage. He spent the following Christmas with the Ayers and discussed it with Beatrice. They settled nothing, but Patton knew that they must decide on something soon, "for I would look like an ass hanging around much longer." [38] He proposed to her in a letter, and they were married in a grand society wedding at Beverly Farms, Massachusetts, in May 1910. After a month of honeymoon-ing, they returned to the Ayer home in Boston and then on to Fort Sheridan to begin—despite the rigors of army life—a very happy marriage. Bea gave birth to their first daughter, Beatrice Jr., nine months later.

While at Fort Sheridan, Patton started writing his first military papers. In one unpublished article, entitled

"National Defense," he expressed his basic philosophy of warfare: "Attack, push forward, attack again until the end."[39] With the help of Bea, who translated French military journals for him and polished his prose, GSP went on to write many articles for the *Cavalry Journal*.

Although his future fame resided in mechanized warfare, Patton never lost sight of the men in the machines. In another treatise he wrote, "We children of a mechanical age are interested and impressed by machines to such an extent that we forget that no machine is better than its operator."[40] His first concern then and always was for his men.

In December 1911, the Pattons relocated with K Troop to Fort Myer, Virginia, where he trained hard to represent the United States in the modern pentathlon at the 1912 Olympic Games in Stockholm, Sweden. Among a field of 47 competitors, he finished fifth in the overall event comprised of fencing, riding, swimming, running, and pistol shooting. Two adjudged misses in the pistol competition— in which he had set an Olympic record of 197 out of a possible 200 in practice—cost him a medal. It is possible that the two bullets scored as misses might have passed through other holes on the target. Patton accepted the ruling of the judges without complaint.

On their return trip to the United States, the Pattons stopped off in France for two weeks where GSP attended the Armor School at Saumur. He received private lessons from the school's Master of Arms, who was the professional fencing champion of Europe. This led to his being picked to return to Saumur in July 1913 to study swordsmanship. He had already been assigned to the Mounted Service School at Fort Riley, Kansas, as a student and also to serve as "Master of the Sword." In the latter capacity, Patton rewrote the U.S. Army's saber manual. "The whole French system of mounted saber fencing," he asserted, "is concentrated in the word: 'Attack!'"[41] Patton held the word in high regard.

After graduating from the cavalry school, Patton continued on at Fort Riley as an instructor. In 1915, Beatrice traveled to California to stay with the Pattons while she gave birth to their second daughter, Ruth Ellen, on February 28. Orders arrived in the autumn of that year sending GSP to Fort Bliss, Texas. Beatrice and the girls returned to the Ayer family home in Beverly, Massachusetts, and the Pattons began another of their many long separations. Patton found himself at the right place at the right time.

By 1915, El Paso had become a hideout for western outlaws and a haven for Mexican border crossers. The town owed its existence in large part to the railroad and to the garrison at Fort Bliss, which was located on the northern outskirts of El Paso. Patton's transfer coincided with a period of steadily worsening relations between the United States and Mexico.

Francisco "Pancho" Villa (Doroteo Arango), a Mexican guerrilla leader, had conducted a series of raids along the U.S.–Mexican border, terrorizing U.S. citizens in Arizona, New Mexico, and Texas. By the end of the year, he had become a major embarrassment to U.S. President Woodrow Wilson. When Villa and his *pistoleros* (gunmen) ransacked the town of Columbus, New Mexico, on March 9, 1916, killing 18 Americans, Wilson authorized Brigadier General John J. Pershing to mount a punitive expedition against the Mexican guerrilla and revolutionary. Patton volunteered to go along as Pershing's aide. A week later, the expedition moved into Mexico.

Pershing failed to capture the elusive Villa, but his soldiers dispersed the Mexican guerrillas and put an end to Villa's border raids. The expedition also served to provide GSP with invaluable soldiering experience. "I have

In 1916, a brutal border raid into New Mexico made by Mexican guerrilla leader Pancho Villa prompted President Woodrow Wilson to send the U.S. army after Villa. George Patton (fifth from left) was then serving under expedition commander General John J. "Black Jack" Pershing (fourth from left). Although the U.S. forces did not capture Villa, they did scatter his guerrillas and end the costly and embarrassing border attacks.

learned more useful soldiering while in Mexico than all the rest of my service put together,"[42] he stated in a letter to Beatrice. He also received his long-awaited promotion to first lieutenant, his first step up the ladder of command, and participated in one of the expedition's more memorable encounters.

On May 14, 1916, Pershing put GSP in charge of a 15-man foraging party and sent them off to purchase corn from neighboring Mexican farmers. They set out in three open touring cars. During their search, a ranch near San Miguelito attracted Patton's attention, and he devised a simple plan on the spot to effectively surround the ranch house using both men and vehicles. Unknown to the Americans, they had stumbled upon the quarters of "General" Julio Cardenas, Pancho Villa's personal bodyguard.

Pursuing Pancho Villa

Starting in 1911, political instability and internal conflicts in the northern part of Mexico led to recurrent incidents along the Mexican border with the United States. The repetitive events posed a danger to U.S. citizens in the border states and threatened to escalate into a full-blown war between the two neighboring countries. President William Howard Taft ordered the strengthening of border patrols and sent an army division to San Antonio, Texas, to hold maneuvers and maintain a presence in the region. Stability returned to the border for the better part of two years.

In 1913, General Victoriano Huerta overthrew and replaced Mexican President Francisco Madera. The deposed president's assassination shortly thereafter resulted in a full-scale civil war between Huerta's forces and two opposing forces—General Venustiano Carranza's constitutionalists, and Emiliano Zapata's radicals. Francisco "Pancho" Villa, an advocate of radical land reform, aligned himself with Carranza but broke with him in 1914 and was forced to flee northward with Zapata.

In 1916, to demonstrate that Carranza did not control the North, Villa initiated a series of border incidents culminating in a surprise raid on March 9 with 500 to 1,000 of his men on Columbus, New Mexico. Villa's guerrillas killed at least 18 Americans and devastated considerable property before the U.S. Thirteenth Cavalry drove them off with a loss of about 100 Villistas. The following day, President Woodrow Wilson ordered Brigadier General John J. Pershing with 10,000 troops—mostly cavalry—into Mexico to assist Carranza's government in capturing Villa.

Despite Pershing's best efforts, Villa's knowledge of the region and his popularity with the Mexican people made him impossible to catch. Worsening relations between the U.S. and Mexican governments—and the imminence of war with Germany—forced Wilson to withdraw Pershing's Punitive Expedition in February 1917. But Pershing's pursuit of Pancho Villa provided excellent training for U.S. Army and National Guard troops whose services would soon be required abroad.

Suddenly, as Patton was positioning his men, three horsemen rode up and began firing at the Americans. Patton, with his ivory-handled Colt 1873 single-action .45-caliber revolver (which he had substituted for his government-issued Colt .45 automatic), shot one of the riders out of the saddle and shot the horse out from under a second rider. When the second rider arose, he fired at Patton and missed. GSP promptly shot him dead. It was Julio Cardenas. The Americans dispatched the third horseman in similar fashion. Patton and his party created quite a stir in Pershing's camp later, when they drove in with their three victims strapped across the blistering-hot hoods of their touring cars.

Patton wrote to Bea about the shoot-out later, confessing that he had been teased "because I used a pistol instead of a saber the other day, but it simply goes to show that an officer should be able to use all arms, for being on foot I could not have used a saber."[43] He went on to add, "The Gen. [Pershing] has been very complimentary telling some officers that I did more in half a day than the 13 Cav. [Thirteenth Cavalry] did in a week."[44] The firefight at San Miguelito constituted the first incident of motorized warfare in the history of the U.S. Army and served as a precursor of things soon to come. And it seems fitting that Patton, the future tank commander, was at the vanguard of a new era.

4

Hallmarks of
Leadership

During the 11-month pursuit of Villa, General Pershing and Lieutenant Patton formed a bond that would last a lifetime. When the United States entered World War I in April 1917 and President Wilson appointed Pershing to lead the American Expeditionary Force (AEF) in Europe, it surprised no one that the general selected Patton as his aide and headquarters commandant. The recently promoted Captain Patton sailed for France with an advance element of the AEF in May.

At Pershing's headquarters in Chaumont, France, Patton's initial enthusiasm over going to war soon wore thin. He quickly tired of his administrative duties and hankered for some real

During their 11 months in Mexico, Pershing (seen here) and Patton formed a strong and enduring bond. When the United States entered World War I, Pershing specifically requested that Patton serve as his aide. Now a captain, Patton was placed in charge of the fledgling American tank training center at Langres, France.

action. In a letter to Bea in September, he wrote:

> There is a lot of talk about "Tanks" here now and I am interested as I can see no future to my present job. . . . It will be a long time yet before we have any [tanks] so don't get worried. . . . I love you too much to try to get killed but also too much to be willing to sit on my tail and do nothing. [45]

Patton approached Pershing for a transfer to a fighting

unit. Fortunately for the U.S. Army, Pershing understood and he posted Patton to organize, train, and command the troops at the American tank training center at Langres. Patton pitched into his new duties with a passion. To become totally familiar and proficient with tanks before opening his school, he spent two weeks at the French tank training center near Compiègne, and another week visiting with British tank units at Cambrai. While he was at Cambrai, the British launched a massive tank attack against the Germans—three brigades and 476 tanks—at Cambrai to usher in the age of armored warfare in the twentieth century.

A few weeks later, Patton—now a major at 31 years of age—opened the 302nd Light Tank Center at Bourg, not far from Langres. By the time he exchanged the gold leafs of a major for the silver leafs of a lieutenant colonel in April 1918, he had become without a doubt the leading tank expert in the AEF. As commander of the newly formed First Tank Brigade, Patton demanded of his troops the highest standards of dress and behavior, requirements that would soon—and ever after—be synonymous with Patton's commands. In one of many memoranda that he issued to his tankers, he outlined his tank priorities:

1. Mobility of strategic employment

2. Speed and radius of action on the battlefield

3. Ease and cheapness of construction

4. Command for the guns and vision

5. Ability to cross trenches. [46]

While most of his contemporaries were obsessed with lengthening tanks to cross wider and wider trenches, Patton was already emphasizing mobility over everything else, the importance of which he would demonstrate in the days ahead—but most dramatically in World War II. His first taste of mobile tank warfare came in September 1918.

Since 1914, the St.-Mihiel salient (protrusion) in the German lines had posed a threat to the Allies—Britain, France, and (from 1917 on) the United States. In September 1918, France's Marshal Ferdinand Foch, supreme commander of the Allied forces, decided to reduce the bulge in the German lines preparatory to an all-out offensive in the Meuse-Argonne sector of the Western Front.

Marshal Foch assigned the task to General Pershing's U.S. First Army, with the French Second Colonial Corps attached. The French 505th Tank Brigade was also to support the assault, upping the total number of tanks to more than 260. Some 3,000-plus artillery pieces and 1,500 aircraft were to render additional support for 16 American infantry divisions.

The Allied plan called for two simultaneous attacks on the salient—one from west to east, the other from the south. Pershing's main effort was to come from the south, with Major General Hunter Liggett's I Corps on the right and Major General Joseph T. Dickman's IV Corps on the left. Meanwhile, the U.S. V Corps would attack from the west while the French Second Colonial Corps mounted a holding action against the town itself. Pershing detailed Patton's First Tank Brigade—later renamed the 304th Tank Brigade—to support Dickman's First Division on the left flank.

Patton's brigade consisted of the 344th Tank Battalion led by Major Sereno Brett and the 345th Tank Battalion under Captain Ranulf Compton—174 tanks in all. Most of the tanks were French-built Renault T 17 six-ton light tanks armed with a 37-mm cannon or two 8-mm

Patton soon found himself in command of two armored battalions. One would lead the U.S. Army's First Infantry Division, while the other would accompany the "Rainbow Division" – so named because its soldiers came from many different states. Using French-built Renault tanks, each battalion was able to rout the enemy and gain its objective before running out of fuel.

Hotchkiss machine guns mounted in a rotating turret. Running with throttles wide open, the little Renaults were capable of reaching blazing speeds of almost six miles an hour.

Patton directed Brett, on the left, to lead the infantry of the U.S. First Division (the "Big Red One") to their objectives near the village of Nonsard. To their right, Compton was to start behind the infantry of the Forty-Second ("Rainbow") Division, then pass through the foot soldiers and lead them in turn into Essey and Pannes. Patton began his custom of issuing a letter of final instructions at St.-Mihiel. In his first final order, of which all such letters were meant to lift troop morale, he wrote:

> No tank is to be abandoned or surrendered to the enemy. If you are left alone in the midst of the enemy keep shooting. If your gun is disabled use your pistols and squash the enemy with your tracks. By quick changes of direction cut them with the tail of your tank. If your motor is stalled and your gun broken still the [enemy] infantry cannot hurt. You hang on, help will come. . . . You must establish the fact that AMERICAN TANKS DO NOT SURRENDER. . . . As long as one tank is able to move it must go forward; its presence will save the lives of hundreds of infantry and kill many Germans. Finally, this is our BIG CHANCE; WHAT WE HAVE WORKED FOR. . . . MAKE IT WORTHWHILE.[47]

At 5:00 A.M. on September 12, 1918, following a four-hour artillery barrage, the First Tank Brigade moved through mud and heavy drizzle into the attack with GSP at its head. From the outset, Patton was forced to face a communications dilemma that would dog him until the advent of radio in World War II.

Colonel Samuel D. Rockenbach, commander of the American Expeditionary Force Tank Corps and GSP's immediate superior, had ordered him to set up a command post to the rear of the action and to stay in contact with his superiors, his reserves, and the supporting artillery at all times. But from the rear, he could neither see nor personally influence the forward action. Characteristically,

Patton elected to lead from the front and to worry about a reprimand later. He later wrote:

> [T]he whole country was alive with [tanks] crawling over trench[es] and into the woods. It was fine but I could not see my right battalion [Compton] so went to look for it; in doing so we passed through several town[s] under shell fire but none did more than throw dust on us. I admit that I wanted to duck and probably did at first but soon saw the futility of dodging fate; besides I was the only officer around who had left on his shoulder straps [bearing rank insignia] and I had to live up to them. It was much easier than you would think and the feeling, foolish probably, of being admired by the men lying down is a great stimulus.[48]

Patton might have added the obvious—that it was also a great risk—but he was for most of his life a fatalist. He felt that he would not get hit unless fate willed it, and in that case there was little he could do about it.

On the road to Essey, with shells flying overhead, he walked toward the sound of guns and ran into Brigadier General Douglas MacArthur, a brigade commander with the Rainbow Division. MacArthur "was standing on a little hill," Patton wrote afterward. "I joined him and the creeping barrage came along toward us. . . . I think each one [of us] wanted to leave, but each [of us] hated to say so, so we let it come over us."[49] GSP added, "We stood and talked but neither [of us] was much interested in what the other said."[50]

At the outskirts of Pannes, dead Germans and horses—the remains of an artillery battalion—littered the road. When Patton arrived, riding atop one of Compton's tanks, he found that two American tanks had halted outside town. They had run out of fuel. Lead elements of infantry from the Forty-Second Division, apparently appalled at the sickening sight, were refusing to enter the village. He ordered his tank into town. A sergeant and a lieutenant joined him on the rear of the tank, and they rolled into Pannes. Inside the town, GSP's two companions jumped off the tank and captured about 30 German prisoners.

On the other side of Pannes, with bullets chinking off the tank and Patton still on top of it, he tapped on the tank's turret with his walking stick and ordered it back to town, leading the way on foot. When four more of Compton's tanks came up, he sent all five tanks through Pannes to attack the next town, Beney. He followed on foot while the tanks stormed the town and seized 4 artillery pieces and 16 machine guns.

Satisfied that Compton's battalion had achieved its objective, Patton turned west and trudged on foot across what had earlier been no-man's-land to look in on the 344th Battalion. He found Brett and 25 of his tanks at Nonsard. They had reached their objective and more, but they had run out of fuel. Patton then turned to the rear to report in to corps HQ and to have gasoline sent forward.

Refueling took place during the night and Patton's brigade moved out again the next morning, with Brett advancing to Vigneuelles; Compton to St. Benoit. With the Germans in full retreat, General Pershing called an end to the fighting. In slightly more than 36 hours, the Americans had reduced the St.-Mihiel salient and reclaimed the territory that the Germans had held for almost four years. They had captured some 15,000 prisoners and 450 guns, while proving themselves a match for any soldiers who fought on French soil. In Pershing's words, "the allies found that they had a formidable army to aid them, and the enemy learned finally that he had one to reckon with."[51]

The Americans paid for their victory with 7,000 casualties. And Patton's part in the stunning American success earned him a reprimand from his corps commander.

At St.-Mihiel, France, this cemetery and memorial bear witness to the many American soldiers who gave their lives here. Although Patton's tanks were able to overcome the challenges of trench warfare and force a German retreat from the area, the victory had its costs.

As Patton confided to Beatrice later, Rockenbach gave him "hell for going up [with the forward elements] but it had to be done. At least I will not sit in a dug out and have my men out in the fighting."[52] In the next war, the radio would resolve the communications problems, both between tanks and between forward and rearward elements. Rockenbach later recommended Patton, as already noted, for two high decorations.

The reduction of the St.-Mihiel salient marked an important milestone in Patton's career. As historian Dale Wilson points out in his consummate study of the Tank Corps, the battle "provided him with a vision of what more mechanically advanced tanks might be able to accomplish on future battlefields operating as an independent combat arm."[53]

Wilson further takes note of Patton's "rare ability to adjust quickly to a rapidly changing situation on the battlefield" and professes that this "trait would later become a hallmark of his World War II operations."[34]

Patton's hallmark traits do not end there. Other qualities that must rank of equal importance were his methods of training for and commanding in combat. His troops always exhibited high morale and discipline, a singular loyalty to their commander, and a peerless will to advance. And when there was a fight to be fought, Patton could always be found in the thick of it. These characteristics are what distinguished his leadership.

5

Full Circle

The severe wound to Patton's thigh and buttock that he received in the subsequent Meuse-Argonne offensive ended his active participation on the battlefield in World War I. In February 1919, he and his tank brigade traveled by train for a camp in Marseilles to board ship for home. The camp commander noted that GSP's brigade was "the best disciplined unit he had seen pass through."[55] Their discipline was, of course, the hallmark of their commander.

Aboard ship, on the long voyage home, Patton took great pains to ensure proper accommodations and food for his troops, fussing over them like his Aunt Nannie had once fussed over him. Upon his arrival in New York in mid-March,

In November 1918, American troops on the front lines near St.-Mihiel cheered the news of an Armistice ending World War I. After being wounded in battle, Patton returned home but found the adjustment difficult—fearing that his chance for greatness had passed him by.

he noted in his diary, "The end of a perfect war. Fini." [56] The next two decades would prove difficult for him.

During the 20 years separating World Wars I and II, Patton would lose his youthful appearance and most of his hair, gain weight, and suffer through a midlife crisis. He would grow to fear that his life and career might pass him by before another war came along. He once complained to his Papa and Mama that "wars were getting scarce and that all the time I had spent getting ready would be wasted for lack of opportunity." [57]

After a promising start in World War I, a serious

wound had cut short his grand ambitions for battlefield greatness. Throughout the 1920s and 1930s, he would hunger for a second chance to blaze a path to personal glory. His time would come, of course. In the interim, he would vent his frustrations and keep in shape on the polo fields of his wealthy family, in-laws, and acquaintances.

In the war's aftermath, a nation weary of war fighting and bloodletting allowed its army to deteriorate. During the war, the Tank Corps had grown to some 20,000 officers and enlisted men. In 1919, the special staff of the War Department—which was charged with reorganizing the army—set the size of the Tank Corps to 154 officers and 2,508 enlisted personnel. The staff also negated the independent status of the Tank Corps and placed it under the control of the Chief of Infantry.

At the end of June 1920, corps commander Samuel D. Rockenbach, who had been promoted to brigadier general, was demoted to colonel, and Patton reverted from acting colonel to a permanent rank of captain. The next day, however, Patton was promoted to major in the regular army. Retaining command of the 304th Tank Brigade— formerly the First—at Camp Meade, Maryland, he began a 20-year climb to flag rank (general or admiral ranking) from there. Patton quickly realized that an emasculated tank corps in a peacetime army was not the best place to further his advancement, so he transferred back into the cavalry. In October 1920, he joined the Third Cavalry at Fort Myer, Virginia, as commanding officer, Third Squadron. (A squadron is equal to a battalion in the infantry.)

Patton's return to the cavalry, his first love, did not mean that he had disdained the future of tanks in modern warfare, for he would devote much of his time to advancing his theories on the new weapons system over the next two decades. He read all the articles about armored warfare in European military journals, and he wrote many articles of his own for the *Cavalry Journal* and other military magazines. His controversial views were not always well received by his colleagues, but his publications kept his name in front of those who could aid his advancement.

While advocating the future of tanks, Patton did not neglect his duties and career path in the cavalry. In 1923, he attended the Field Officers' Course in Fort Riley, Kansas, and the Command and General Staff College at Fort Leavenworth, Kansas. On Christmas Eve of that year, Beatrice presented him with the son that he had always wanted, George Smith Patton IV. Civilian Joe Angelo, who had saved Patton's life in the Meuse-Argonne, wrote to congratulate his former commander and to "hope [the baby] will some day be an officer like his father."[58] Patton, now 38 years old, completed the staff course the following June as an honor graduate and went on to staff appointments in Boston (1924) and in Hawaii (1925–1928).

In 1928, Patton returned to the mainland and joined the Office of the Chief of Cavalry in Washington, D.C., where he directed the rewriting of the army manual on the pistol. Three years later, in 1932, he attended the Army War College, also in Washington. He finished the course as a "distinguished graduate." That same year, the army awarded him a much-belated Purple Heart for the wound he received in World War I. In July, he returned to Fort Myer, this time to serve as executive officer of the Third Cavalry. On March 1, 1932, he again pinned on the silver oak leaf clusters of a lieutenant colonel, and a year later, he sailed for a second tour of duty in Hawaii. This time, Patton served as director of the G-2 (intelligence) section of the Hawaiian Department, under Major General Hugh A. Drum at Fort Shafter.

As the director of G-2, Patton focused on the security of the Hawaiian Islands and their vulnerability to attack.

Between the World Wars, Patton completed his military education at the Command and General Staff College in Fort Leavenworth, Kansas. During the 1920s, he went on to serve appointments in Boston and Hawaii. It was during this time that his son, George Smith Patton IV, was born.

Having tracked Japan's occupation of Manchuria in 1931 and its invasion of China in 1933, he became convinced that a war between Japan and the United States was inevitable. In a chilling article entitled "Surprise," he theorized on the likelihood of "the unheralded arrival during a period of profound peace of a Japanese expeditionary force within 200 miles of Oahu during darkness; this force to be preceded by submarines who will be in the immediate vicinity of Pearl Harbor."[59]

His article went on to predict the sabotage of key military installations and the assassination of commanding officers. Moreover, it described the potential for "an air attack by [Japanese] navy fighters and carrier borne

Professional Men-at-Arms

George S. Patton Jr. was every inch a soldier and a leader. He was always keenly aware of the responsibilities of rank. In a lecture given to his subordinates shortly after World War I, Patton defined "The Obligation of Being an Officer." In his speech—as quoted in Martin Blumenson's *The Patton Papers, 1885–1940*—he declared in part:

[W]e, as officers of the army, are not only members of the oldest of honorable professions, but are also the modern representatives of the demi-gods (almost divine beings) and heroes of antiquity.

Back of us stretches a line of men whose acts of valor, of self-sacrifice and of service have been the theme of song and story since long before recorded history began. . . .

In the days of chivalry—the golden age of our profession— knights-officers were noted as well for courtesy and gentleness of behavior, as for death-defying courage. . . . From their acts of courtesy and benevolence was derived the word, now pronounced as one, Gentle Man. . . . Let us be GENTLE. That is, courteous and considerate of the rights of others. Let us be MEN. That is, fearless and untiring in doing our duty as we see it.

[O]ur calling is most ancient and like all other old things it has amassed through the ages certain customs and traditions which decorate and ennoble it, which render beautiful the otherwise prosaic occupation of being professional men-at-arms: Killers.

bombers on air stations and the submarine base using either gas or incendiary bombs."[60] GSP's prophetic paper failed to alarm those ultimately responsible for the defense of the Islands, and his warning treatise died of inattention.

Frustrated by a series of staff assignments that confined him to a desk and by his ever-growing fear of failing to achieve his career goals, Patton succumbed to a midlife crisis that threatened to destroy both his marriage and his career. At 53 years of age, his self-esteem hit bottom. He fell subject to frequent fits of anger and mood swings. To make up for his self-perceived failures, he started drinking heavily and womanizing, often making a fool of himself.

Only the unshakable devotion of his adoring Beatrice held their marriage together. "Your father needs me," she told their daughter Ruth Ellen after GSP had engaged in a romantic indiscretion. "He doesn't know it right now, but he needs me. In fact, right now he needs me more than I need him."[61] Her loyalty when lesser women might have bolted perhaps demonstrated that army wives also know something about honor and duty. In any case, the Pattons survived GSP's midlife crisis and returned to the mainland in June 1937.

The Pattons looked forward to a long leave before reporting again to Fort Riley, Kansas, where GSP was to serve as executive officer of the Academic Division of the Cavalry School and Ninth Cavalry. Far from a pleasant diversion, however, their vacation turned into a near-career-ending disaster for Patton.

While riding with Beatrice, her horse suddenly bolted and kicked him in the leg, snapping it like a matchstick. A blood clot or air bubble in his bloodstream brought him close to death, hospitalizing him for three months and confining him at home for three more. He finally reported to Fort Riley in February 1938, still limping and wearing an iron brace on his leg. But through systematic exercising, he worked himself back to good health and fitness.

On July 1, Patton was promoted to full colonel. After 20 years, he had at last regained the highest rank that he had held during World War I. Advancement in the peacetime army had not come easy for GSP, and he had begun to think about retirement. But a new posting in late July breathed new life into his career aspirations. On July 24, he reported to Fort Clark, Texas, to take command of the Fifth Cavalry. Fort Clark, near Eagle Pass and the Mexican border, was a sleepy backwater post where the army sent old cavalrymen to finish out their careers in peace and quiet. But Patton did not mind. He was back in the cavalry.

After the briefest assignment of his career, Patton struck Fort Clark like a Texas tornado, demanding spit and polish and strict discipline, declaring the cavalry obsolete, and experimenting with new organizational and operational concepts. He had been sent to Fort Clark to take part in a series of maneuvers conducted by the Third Army in Texas, and he participated in his own freewheeling style. Once, while maneuvering in the desert, a mock enemy artillery colonel refused to surrender to one of his captains, Patton rode up "and stuck my white pistol in his face then he was very quiet." [62]

Patton enjoyed the assignment immensely, but it ended quickly as well. In December, he received a phone call from Major General John Herr informing him that he was being reassigned to Fort Myer and command of the Third Cavalry. He was to replace Colonel Jonathan Wainwright (who would later gain fame as the defender of Bataan and Corregidor in the Philippines). Unlike the privately wealthy Pattons, Wainwright had no outside source of income. He could no longer bear the expense of lavish entertaining that was required of the commanding officer of Washington's showcase military installation.

Patton exploded upon hearing the news and blamed Beatrice's money for yanking him away from real soldiering at Fort Clark and wrecking his career. Although he loved Fort Myer, he wanted no part of the glad-handing Washington social whirl. "A lot of very fancy language got thrown around as we packed," Ruth Ellen recalled later, "and Ma got her feelings hurt."[63] The Patton household remained unsettled for some time to come.

The irate Patton received some consolation before leaving Texas when a board of officers examined him and qualified him eligible for promotion to brigadier general. And Brigadier General Kenyon A. Joyce, base commander at Fort Clark, rated GSP "superior" and "an outstanding leader who has great mental and physical energy. Because of his innate dash and great physical courage and endurance he is a cavalry officer from whom extraordinary feats might be expected in war."[64] Kenyon's staunch assessment of Patton's wartime potential helped GSP to keep alive his dreams of future glory.

Patton's transfer to command at Fort Myer served not to devastate his career but rather to enhance it. In the spring of 1939, GSP began cultivating the friendship of General George C. Marshall, who, as the army's new acting chief of staff, resided at Fort Myer. Marshall, although immune to flatterers, recognized Patton's unique qualities and strengths. He became further impressed with GSP's leadership during maneuvers in Virginia that summer. Marshall's permanent appointment as chief of staff coincided with the outbreak of World War II in Europe on September 1.

On that September morning, the forces of German dictator Adolf Hitler, which included 10 armored divisions

Though not suited to a desk job, Patton reluctantly held a series of staff appointments. It was while serving as commander of Fort Myer that Patton forged a friendship with General George C. Marshall (seen here). With the outbreak of World War II, Marshall became Army Chief of Staff, and Patton would again find himself where he felt most at home—commanding tanks.

and some 1,600 close-support aircraft, stormed across the frontier of Poland. In just 17 days, Hitler's armies— seeking more *Lebensraum* (living space) for Germans— overpowered the courageous but obsolete Polish Army. And a new word entered the lexicon of modern warfare— *blitzkrieg* (lightning war)!

Patton studied the press accounts of this new kind of accelerated mechanized warfare with intense interest. He began to rethink his old views on the use of tanks as a support arm of the infantry. This new form of lightning war rendered the old concepts as outmoded as horse-drawn artillery. As he pondered the emerging formations and tactics of rapid advance, he began to question his ability to function effectively as a leader in an environment unlike any that he had trained for over the years. If he wondered whether he himself was obsolete, he was about to find out.

In the spring of 1940, Patton served as an umpire during Third Army maneuvers in Texas. Mechanized elements confronted horse cavalry units and so outperformed them that the need for drastic army modernization became painfully apparent. And while the Germans were overrunning western Europe, defeating France and forcing the British off the continent, the maneuvers enabled Patton to become updated on the latest equipment, developments, and thinking of American tankers. He left Texas convinced that machines had supplanted the role of horses in the modern-day army.

The results of the Third Army maneuvers also convinced chief of staff Marshall of the need for modernizing the army. On June 4, he ordered the establishment of a new Armored Force and appointed Brigadier General Adna R. Chaffee Jr. to head it. Patton wrote to Chaffee at once. The letter has since been lost, but GSP apparently had asked to become a part of the new mechanized force.

Chaffee replied that he would place Patton on the "preferred list" as an armored brigade commander, adding, "I need just such a man of your experience in command of an armored brigade. With two light armored regiments and a regiment of tanks employed in a mobile way, I think you could go to town." [65] Whatever

Patton wrote, his letter to Chaffee led directly to his post-ing as commander of the Second Armored Brigade of the Second Armored Division at Fort Benning, Georgia.

Twenty years after World War I, Colonel George S. Patton Jr. had regained his wartime rank and was now back in tanks, once again on track to future glory. His career had come full circle.

6

Rungs of the Ladder

The imminence of war and fate combined to accelerate Patton's advancement. He arrived at Fort Benning to assume command of the Second Armored Brigade on July 26, 1940. His immediate superior was Charles L. Scott, commanding general of the Second Armored Division. In September, Scott moved to Fort Knox, Kentucky, to take command of the First Armored Corps. His transfer was intended to free General Chaffee—who was then ailing with cancer—to concentrate on developing the Armored Force. A month later, Patton's promotion to brigadier general finally came through, and he was appointed acting commanding general of the Second Armored Division in November. In a letter to Terry de la Mesa Allen, an old polo-playing friend who was also

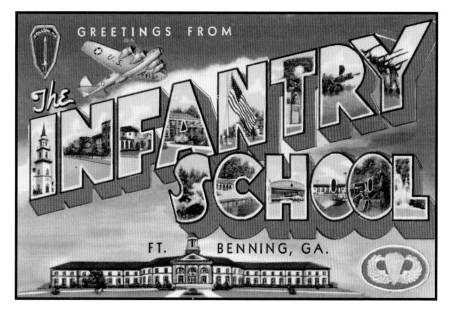

In July 1940, Patton arrived at Fort Benning, Georgia, to assume command of the Second Armored Brigade. Now a brigadier general, Patton would use this time to make his understaffed and ill-equipped division ready for battle. This vintage postcard from 1942 shows the main building of the Infantry School at Ft. Benning, Georgia.

promoted to brigadier general, Patton wrote, "[A]ll that is now needed is a nice juicy war."[66]

War would come in due course, but in the meantime Patton first needed to whip his woefully understaffed and ill-equipped division into fighting shape. His task was great, as evidenced by his own words. "I have sixteen thousand men [many of them draftees] who have never seen an officer," he said, "and twelve hundred officers who have never seen a man—so I have quite a job on my hands."[67] Patton set about his task with his usual vigor.

In a lecture to his officers, Patton cited Julius Caesar, who trained his Roman legions so well in the winter that they knew precisely what to do on their own in their spring campaigns. "This [is] . . . exactly the goal we are seeking in this division," he said. "I know that we shall attain it and when we do, may God have mercy on our enemies; they will need it."[68]

To achieve this goal, Patton led by example and established himself as a role model. He demanded strict discipline and strenuous training. Setting high standards, he personally ensured that they were attained. Most important, he constantly praised their development and accomplishments, thereby instilling personal pride, esprit de corps, and high morale.

In April 1941, after eight months of intensive training, Patton noted, "We have changed from an idea to a powerful fighting force."[69] His superiors agreed, rewarding him with the second star of a major general and appointing him permanent—rather than acting—commander of the division that he had trained so well. Throughout the rest of the year, Patton's division maintained its combat readiness with a series of maneuvers—in Tennessee in June, in Louisiana-Texas in August and September, and in North Carolina in October and November.

On December 5, General Scott congratulated Patton and his troops "for the esprit de corps, the energy, the endurance, the initiative, and the fine fighting spirit"[70] that they displayed during the maneuvers. Two days later, on Sunday morning, December 7, 1941, the Japanese launched a surprise attack on Pearl Harbor and other U.S. military installations in Hawaii and the Philippines. The next day, the United States declared war on Japan. Three days later, Germany and Italy declared war on the United States.

The United States joined with Great Britain and the Soviet Union to form the principal nations known as the Allies, and went to war against Germany, Italy, and Japan, the chief member nations of the so-called Axis Powers. The "nice juicy war" that Patton had spent two decades preparing for had begun.

Army chief of staff Marshall immediately sent General

While at Fort Benning, Patton once commented that all he needed was "a nice juicy war." He got that and more when the Japanese launched a surprise air attack against the U.S. Pacific Fleet at Pearl Harbor, Hawaii, on Sunday morning, December 7, 1941. The attack resulted in shocking losses for the navy and signaled America's entrance into the war.

Scott to the Middle East as an observer. In mid-January of 1942, Marshall appointed Patton to command the First Armored Corps in place of Scott. But the next month, Patton received orders to form and direct a desert training center in a remote desert region near Riverside, California. Erwin Rommel and his German and Italian armies in Libya were then threatening to overrun the Suez Canal. The Americans faced the possibility of having to support the British in North Africa and needed realistic training and rugged conditioning.

Despite fears that being stuck away in another back-water post might cause his superiors to overlook him for a combat role, Patton—always loyal and dedicated—again delivered the kind of tough training for which he had become so well known.

Patton now reported to two bosses. As commander of the First Armored Corps, he answered to Lieutenant General Jacob L. Devers, who had taken command of the Armored Force upon General Chaffee's death (from cancer) in August 1941. Devers was an old West Point classmate of Patton's. As director of the Desert Training Center, he came under Lieutenant General Lesley J. McNair, who was responsible for troop training. To keep his name in front of both men, Patton wrote voluminous reports to each. He let Devers know in the strongest terms that he wanted to fight and not be consigned to a training operation. And he candidly informed McNair that when serious fighting started he wanted the chance "to prove in blood what I have learned in sweat."[71] His opportunity came sooner than he had expected.

On July 30, after President Franklin D. Roosevelt had decided with British Prime Minister Winston Churchill to mount an Allied invasion of North Africa, General McNair, General Marshall's chief of staff, summoned Patton to Washington. McNair, with the concurrence of General Devers, had selected Patton to lead the first contingent of Americans to fight on the European side of the Atlantic Ocean in World War II.

The Americans had wanted to invade Europe but ultimately agreed with the British to defer a continental operation until the two nations could assemble a stronger invasion force. Meanwhile, the North African campaign would appease Soviet leader Joseph Stalin's demands for a second front and tie up Axis forces that Hitler might otherwise deploy against the Soviets. In any case, Patton's persistent reporting and letter writing to his two bosses had paid off handsomely.

When Patton arrived in Washington, he set up his headquarters in the Munitions Building on Constitution Avenue. There, he first learned about Operation TORCH, the plan-in-work for the Allied invasion of French North Africa. Lieutenant General Dwight D. "Ike" Eisenhower had been selected to command the joint Anglo-American operation. Eisenhower and Patton had served together briefly after World War I. They had grown to like each other and had remained friends over the years.

On August 5, Patton flew to London to confer with Eisenhower and other Allied leaders about his role in the planned operation and to garner an overall perspective on the plan called TORCH. Patton, happy to be reunited with his old friend and cheerful at the prospect of returning to combat, spent three weeks in England. Before leaving, he told his friend of his intention "to succeed or die in the attempt."[72]

The final plan called for simultaneous landings at three points—in Morocco near the Atlantic port of Casablanca, and in Algeria near the ports of Oran and Algiers. The Western Task Force under Patton—35,000 men in 39 vessels—was to sail directly from the United States to Morocco. Major General Lloyd R. Fredendall's Central Task Force—39,000 men and 47 ships—would depart from England and land at Oran. And the Eastern Task Force under Major General Charles W. Ryder—33,000 men and 34 ships—would also sail from England but land near Algiers. Except for the Royal Navy and a British contingent with Ryder's force, the invasion of North Africa was to be primarily an American operation.

After securing their initial objectives, the Allied invaders were to race eastward to secure Tunisia before German and Italian forces could move in. At the same time, the British Eighth Army under General Bernard L. Montgomery was to advance westward to crush Field Marshal Erwin Rommel's German and Italian armies in a vise and eject them from the continent. D day—the start date for the operation—was set for November 8.

The U.S. invasion of North Africa pitted American forces against Moroccan, Algerian, and French soldiers loyal to the French Vichy government, a puppet of Hitler's Nazi regime. Here, American soldiers rounded up Moroccan natives after the U.S. landing at Fedala, Morocco, on November 27, 1942.

With scarcely three months to prepare for the landings, the army had to scramble to get all its forces assembled and ready to deploy. The plan's many complexities were further complicated by the fact that the enemies of all three task forces were not Germans or Italians but French. When France fell to the Germans on June 25, 1940, the French had pledged to sit out the rest of the war. In return, the Germans allowed the French to keep most of southern France and their colonial holdings nominally intact under the rule of the collaborative Vichy government. French forces in North Africa were sworn to the Vichy government and bound by the terms of the June armistice to defend Morocco and Algeria against any Allied invasion attempts.

Prior to the landings, the Allies tried through secret negotiations with the French in North Africa to enlist French sympathies and encourage them not to resist the invasion forces. But they had no way of knowing in advance whether the French defenders would resist or lay down their arms when the first Americans splashed ashore. In every case but one, the French resisted.

On the evening of October 23, Patton confided to his diary: "This is my last night in America. It may be for years and it may be forever. God grant that I do my full duty to my men and myself."[73] The next day, Patton and his Western Task Force set sail eastward from Norfolk, Virginia, on a two-week voyage to North Africa.

On November 6, with 40 hours to go before the landings, Patton again reflected somberly in his diary, "[I]t seems that my whole life has been pointed to this moment. When this job is done, I presume I will be pointed to the next step in the ladder of destiny. If I do my full duty, the rest will take care of itself."[74] Duty, Honor, Country—the credo of West Pointers—never left his thoughts for long. They were the rungs of the ladder.

7

The Wages of Duty

To do his full duty, that is, to capture Casablanca and to establish it as the main railhead for resupplying the army in North Africa, Patton split his ground forces—the U.S. Third and Ninth Infantries and Second Armored Divisions—into three elements: One element was to make the main landing at Fedala, a small fishing port about 15 miles north of Casablanca; a second element was to land at Mehdia, 50 miles farther north, to capture the critical airfield at Port Lyautey; and a third component was to storm ashore at Safi, 150 miles south of Casablanca, to fend off the strong French garrison at Marrakesh.

During the Atlantic crossing, Patton read the *Koran* to prepare himself for his forthcoming role in Morocco. He called

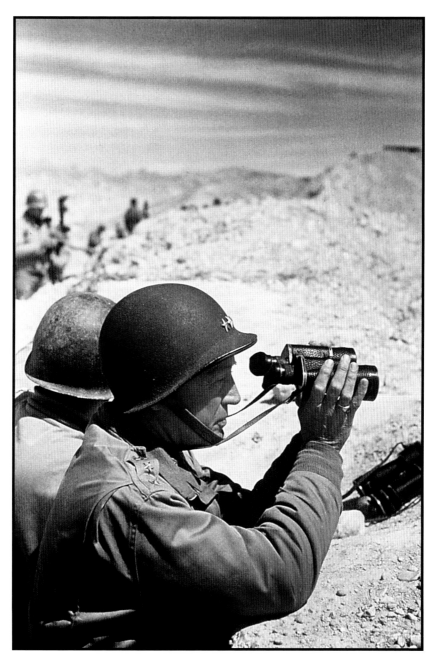

Patton was instrumental in rousing his men to action on the beachheads of North Africa. After crushing French resistance in Morocco and Algeria, U.S. forces had to hurry to reach Tunisia, where British forces had confronted Rommel's tanks.

it "a good book and interesting."[75] Shortly before the Western Task Force invasion fleet reached its destination, Patton ordered a letter to be read to his troops. It said, in part, in a Napoleonic style:

> When the great day of battle comes, remember your train-ing . . . you must succeed—for to retreat is as cowardly as it is fatal. Americans do not surrender.
>
> During the first days and nights ashore . . . you must work unceasingly, regardless of sleep, regardless of food. A pint of sweat will save a gallon of blood.
>
> The eyes of the world are watching us; the heart of America beats for us; God is with us. On our victory depends the freedom or slavery of the human race. We shall surely win.[76]

Under the overall command of General Eisenhower, all three task forces started their runs to shore before daybreak on November 8. General Montgomery's Eighth Army had already repulsed an Axis attack on October 23 and had mounted a counteroffensive that resulted in a stunning British victory at the Egyptian coastal village of El Alamein on November 4. Farther west, Algiers fell to General Ryder's Eastern Task Force in a single day. General Fredendall's Central Task Force met stronger resistance at Oran but compelled the French to capitulate in two days. Patton's Western Task Force encountered the stiffest opposition of all at Casablanca.

The overmatched French Navy met the U.S. fleet and inflicted some damage on the American vessels, but it took a terrible pounding in return. Patton's personal arrival on shore was delayed when French naval gunfire destroyed his landing craft while it still hung from its davits (hoist) aboard the flagship cruiser *Augusta*. Fedala fell at 8:00 A.M. At noon, GSP received a delayed message that Safi had fallen almost seven hours earlier. When he finally reached the beach at 1:20 P.M., in the midst of random incoming fire, he found the shore parties digging foxholes rather than performing their assigned functions. Cursing and prodding, he stirred them to action.

When a landing craft capsized in the rough surf, drowning 16 soldiers, Patton waded into the crashing waves and recovered one of their bodies. One frightened soldier threw himself down on the sand and started sobbing. Patton revitalized him. As GSP later described the episode, he "kicked him in the fanny with all my might and he jumped right up and went to work. Some way to boost morale."[77] He admonished a lieutenant who was reluctant to order his men into the water. And he hit one slacker who was too lazy to push a grounded boat off the sand. Under Patton's gruff leadership, the landing operations soon began operating smoothly. The lone British liaison officer present noted later that Patton's personal effort displayed "a touch of magic."[78]

In Casablanca, the French forces under Governor-General Auguste Noguès held out for three days but surrendered on the fourth day, November 11. In his diary that day, Patton wrote: "I said I would take Casa by D plus 3, and I did. A nice birthday present."[79] At 57 years of age, fame was beginning to find him. Back home, reports from the battlefront were starting to make his name a household word.

The fighting in Morocco cost the Americans 1,280 casualties—530 dead, 650 wounded, and 100 missing. French losses numbered much higher. The French agreed to take up arms on the Allied side, but their resistance had delayed the Allied race to Tunisia. As a result, the Germans poured men, tanks, and planes across the narrow body of water separating Sicily and North Africa, temporarily thwarting an Allied advance on Tunisia.

In January 1943, more than 100,000 troops under German Colonel General Hans Jürgen von Arnim faced Eisenhower's Allied forces in the west. In the east, Field Marshal Rommel's Italian-German army had recoiled from his defeat at El Alamein and stood entrenched in old French fortifications along the Mareth Line in southern Tunisia. Eisenhower had no choice but to dig in and defend the Tunisian mountains until he could coordinate a new attack from both the east and the west.

After Patton's success at Casablanca, Eisenhower relegated him to overseeing the work needed to turn Casablanca into a first-rate supply base. He also charged GSP with fostering good diplomatic relations with the French and Moroccans. Patton did not relish the assignment but diligently discharged his duties, still convinced that destiny would guide his steps up the ladder to high command and battlefield renown. Fate—and Erwin Rommel—took a hand in his climb to greatness in February 1943.

Before the Allies could regroup their forces and resume their converging attacks on the German-Italian armies in Tunisia, Rommel launched a blitzkrieg-type attack against General Fredendall's U.S. Second Corps. The German commander—known as the "Desert Fox" for his prowess in desert operations—quickly broke through the thinly held American positions at Kasserine Pass in west-central Tunisia. And unseasoned American troops broke and ran.

One American colonel reported that he was "just shifting positions," but a second American colonel, Thomas Drake, snorted, "Shifting positions, hell! I know panic when I see it."[80] Eisenhower quickly dispatched four battalions of artillery, which, with the aid of British tanks, forced Rommel's retirement—but not before the U.S. Army suffered one of its most humiliating

German General Erwin Rommel was a dogged warrior and shrewd strategist, characteristics that earned him the nickname the "Desert Fox." Defeating Rommel required a combined effort from U.S. and British armored forces in what amounted to a running tank battle across the desert.

defeats. After Kasserine, Eisenhower relieved Fredendall and named Patton as his replacement as commander of Second Corps.

On March 9, Rommel left North Africa, hoping to

pursuade Hitler and Italian dictator Benito Mussolini to withdraw the Axis troops and thus spare them from what he perceived as their inevitable extinction. Both dictators

The Battle of Kasserine Pass

On February 14, 1943, the German Fifth *Panzer* (Tank) Army under Colonel-General Hans Jürgen von Arnim broke through the positions of Major General Lloyd R. Fredendall's inexperienced U.S. Second Corps at Sidi Bou Zid in Tunisia. Arnim's attack isolated one element of Major General Orlando Ward's First Armored Division and badly mauled two others when Ward counterattacked the next day.

At the same time, to the southwest, an assault group of Field Marshal Erwin Rommel's *Deutsches Afrika Korps* (German Africa Corps) broke through at Gafsa and Thelepte. Rommel advanced rapidly to Kasserine Pass, in the Memetcha Mountains, where he was joined by part of Arnim's Tenth Panzer Division before attacking the U.S. Second Corps.

When the Axis forces attacked through the Kasserine Pass – a two-mile-wide pass between two 4,000-foot-high mountains – Fredendall failed to seize effective control of the battle. Some of his units fled in panic. But British First Army commander Lieutenant General Kenneth Anderson rushed Allied reinforcements into blocking positions on the Thala and Sbiba roads, where they succeeded in halting further thrusts by Arnim's Tenth and Twenty-First Panzer Divisions. To the southwest, the U.S. First Armored Division rallied and checked the advance of Rommel's Afrika Korps assault forces east of Tebessa.

On February 22 – facing poor terrain for mobile operations, increased Allied resistance, and a lack of cooperation from Arnim – Rommel withdrew artfully to prepare for a similar operation against General Bernard L. Montgomery's British Eighth Army on the Mareth Line to the east.

The U.S. Second Corps lost 2,816 dead and wounded, another 2,459 missing in action or captured, and much valuable equipment in one of the most embarrassing losses in the U.S. Army's history. Axis losses totaled about 2,000. Despite the embarrassing loss, the Second Corps reoccupied its lost territory on February 24, and the defeat had no lasting effect on the Allied campaign in North Africa.

denied his pleas. Moreover, because Rommel was suffering from violent headaches and nervous exhaustion, Hitler ordered him to stay in Germany for treatment. Arnim assumed overall command in North Africa and Rommel never returned.

Three days after Rommel's departure, Patton received the third star of a lieutenant general. Unknown to Patton at the time, fate had denied him the chance to go one-on-one against the Desert Fox on the sands of North Africa. But there were still 200,000 enemies left to fight, and he began at once to galvanize his corps for action, improving discipline, dress, and the condition of weapons. Like a blast of desert wind, he tore through every battalion of all four of his divisions, boosting morale and instilling "an adequate hatred of Germans."[81]

On March 15, Second Corps stood poised and ready to attack. Patton's mission was to advance from the Western to the Eastern Dorsale Mountains, seize Gafsa, a town on the road leading to Gabès, then secure the Maknassy defile. The Allies hoped to lure General von Arnim into committing his reserves at Gafsa, rather than at the Mareth Line when Montgomery—directed by British commander in chief General Sir Harold R.L.G. Alexander—resumed his offensive.

That evening, Patton informed his staff: "Gentlemen, tomorrow we attack. If we are not victorious, let no one come back alive."[82] He then retired to his room to pray.

The god of war smiled on Patton and his corps during the ensuing operation that is sometimes called the Battle of El Guettar. Major General Terry de la Mesa Allen's First Infantry Division (nicknamed the "Big Red One") overran Gafsa on March 17, then stormed ten miles down the road to Gabès to seize El Guettar. Allen's success pleased Patton immensely, but GSP grew concerned when the advance of Major General Orlando Ward's First Armored Division stalled at Maknassy. He called Ward and ordered him to get off his backside, grab a pistol in his hand, and lead his division forward.

Years later, Omar N. Bradley, who served as Patton's chief of staff in Tunisia, recalled the incident: "Ward did lead a night attack [on March 24] at the head of his infantry . . . [and] was slightly wounded in the eye. He probably would have preferred to have been killed that night."[83] Patton awarded Ward the Silver Star for his action, later commenting that it warranted the Distinguished Service Cross "except for the fact that it was necessary for me to order him to do it."[84]

On April 1, the daily Situation Report—called "Sitrep"—for Second Corps noted that the corps area had been "continuously bombed all morning"[85] by German aircraft. The reason, as stated in the Sitrep, was: "Total lack of air cover for our [ground] units has allowed German air force to operate at will."[86] The Sitrep was sent to higher and adjacent headquarters. Patton sent out the same message over his own signature.

When Air Marshal Arthur Coningham, Alexander's air officer, read the Sitrep and Patton's affirmation of it, he became irate. He responded in kind. Calling the accusation inherent in the two messages "a false cry of wolf," Coningham suggested that "it can only be assumed that II Corps personnel concerned are not battleworthy in terms of the present operation."[87] This, of course, infuriated Patton, and he demanded a written apology.

Patton raised such a furor over Coningham's demeaning of Second Corps troops that he almost caused a serious rift in Anglo-American relations. Three air force generals arrived at Second Corps headquarters a few days later to assuage Patton. While the four generals conferred, four German Focke-Wulf 190 fighter-bombers roared in over Patton's HQ strafing and bombing. No one was injured in their meeting room, but plaster from the ceiling flaked down on the generals and the door slammed shut from a bomb concussion. The attack seemed to bear out Patton's contention that German planes operated "at will."

One air force general turned to Patton and yelled over the din, "Now how in hell did you ever manage to stage that?"[88]

Patton shouted back, "I'll be damned if I know, but if I could find the sonsabitches who flew those planes I'd mail them each a medal."[89]

Apologies were exchanged shortly afterward between Coningham and Patton, but Eisenhower advised Patton to express his feelings on matters critical to another service in a "confidential report to the next military superior *only*."[90] Allied air support improved.

After El Guettar fell with unanticipated suddenness, Patton, with Alexander's authorization, seized an opportunity to press on to a great victory on the Gabès plain. He ordered a task force from the First Armored Division under Colonel Clarence C. Benson to thrust forward to the coast at Gabès. But Benson made only minimal progress while losing 13 tanks to strong German resistance. Patton finally drove to Benson's headquarters and told him to "keep pushing for a fight or a bath"[91] in the Mediterranean.

Soon afterward, when Benson's leading elements stopped in front of a mine field, Patton flew into a rage. With only a jeep and a scout car in front of him, Patton drove through the mines and led Benson's task force down the road. In his diary entry for April 7, Patton wrote: "Shortly after I turned back, Benson's advance guard made contact with a patrol of the . . . Eighth Army. As it was, I had no idea they [the British] were around and was simply doing my duty as I saw it."[92] Benson's force—with some prodding by GSP—succeeded in capturing more than 1,000 prisoners.

Allied troops in North Africa had more than Rommel's tanks to deal with. Repeated air strikes from Nazi planes caused Patton to demand improved air cover from U.S. and British forces. Here we see a U.S. soldier in his foxhole in Tunisia.

On April 15, 1943, Eisenhower relieved Patton and turned over the operational command of Second Corps to GSP's deputy, Omar Bradley. Ike had never intended for Patton to stay with Second Corps longer than was necessary for him to reestablish its confidence and fighting spirit. Patton had done that. His victory at Gafsa had taken some of the sting out of the American defeat at Kasserine. Three weeks later, the Allies forced the surrender of the Axis armies in Tunis, and the Axis hold on North Africa ended. The Tunisian venture cost the fledgling U.S. Army 18,221 casualties, including 2,715 dead.

Meanwhile, Patton returned to Morocco to resume planning for the next operation on the Allied timetable — the invasion of Sicily. Eisenhower had already designated him to command the U.S. Seventh Army, an upgraded version of the First Armored Corps. In a 43-day stint with Second Corps he had boosted his own confidence and proven again his ability to succeed. With a third star gleaming on his collar, GSP looked forward to his next battle, convinced more than ever that a glorious destiny awaited him. "If I do my duty," he wrote, "I will be paid in the end."[93]

8

Summer in Sicily

Although Patton felt that British overall commander General Sir Harold R.L.G. Alexander had limited the role of the U.S. Second Corps in the final days of the North African campaign—thus denying the Americans an opportunity for a glorious victory—he returned to Morocco in fine spirits. "I have been gone 43 days," he noted in his diary, "fought several successful battles, commanded 95,800 men, lost about ten pounds, gained a third star and a hell of a lot of poise and confidence, and am otherwise the same."[94]

He regretted having to leave Tunisia before the final push to Tunis but chalked up his departure to fate, "who is forging me for some future bigger role."[95] The setting for his next role

In January 1943, President Franklin Roosevelt (seated left) and British Prime Minister Winston Churchill (seated right) and their staffs met at the historic Allied conference at Casablanca. There the decision was made to send Allied troops from North Africa into Europe via Sicily.

lay in Sicily. And the part that he played there in three regrettable acts would almost bring down the curtain on his military career.

Sicily represented the next milestone along the Allied road to Berlin. The decision to invade Sicily had been made by British Prime Minister Churchill and U.S. President Franklin D. Roosevelt and their staffs at the Casablanca Conference in January 1943. Their decision followed from their recognition that the Allied forces still were not ready for a direct thrust across the English Channel. Instead, they devised an interim strategy.

By invading Sicily with troops already available in North Africa, the Allies stood to accomplish three things: First, they would make the Mediterranean safer for Allied shipping; second, they would secure a stepping-stone from which to invade Italy itself; and third, their success in Sicily would potentially force Italy out of the war. As an added plus, they would continue to divert Axis troops that might be used against the Soviets on the Eastern Front. The Allies code-named the Sicilian invasion plan Operation HUSKY.

General Eisenhower, now wearing the four stars of a full general, continued to serve as supreme commander for the operation. Directly under Ike, General Alexander headed the Fifteenth Army Group and served as the operational commander of the ground forces. He controlled Montgomery's British Eighth Army and Patton's newly formed U.S. Seventh Army. Patton's army consisted of the HQ group of Second Corps, four infantry divisions (First, Third, Ninth, and Forty-Fifth), the Second Armored Division, the Eighty-Second Airborne Division, and three Ranger battalions (First, Third, and Fourth).

The principal objective of the Sicilian campaign was Messina, a seaport in northeast Sicily. It stood as the gateway between the narrow body of water separating the three-cornered island from Italy. The Strait of Messina represented the escape route to the Italian mainland for the Axis forces on the island. But the strait was so narrow and heavily fortified that Allied strategists felt that it might be disastrous to attack Messina directly. They therefore planned to conduct landings elsewhere, followed by converging advances along shallow coastal shelves on either side of lofty Mount Etna.

Alexander, employing the principle of mass—the concentration of combat power at the decisive place and time—directed both armies to land in the southeastern corner of the island—the British on the east coast, the Americans on the southwest. Before the main landings, airborne and glider elements were to secure strategic objectives behind the beaches, such as bridges and airfields. Once ashore, Montgomery would mount the main offensive up the east coast, while Patton—much to his dislike—was to execute a blocking action against Axis reserves in the northwest. The Allies set D day as July 10, 1943.

While still at sea, Patton sent another of his now customary messages to his men, stressing honor and urging them to cover themselves in glory:

> We are indeed honored to have been selected for . . . this new and greater attack against the Axis. . . . When we land we will meet German and Italian soldiers whom it is our honor and privilege to attack and destroy. . . . The glory of American arms, the honor of our country, the future of the world rests in your hands.[96]

On the night before the landing, Patton invited his chaplain to his cabin after supper to pray with him. Their prayers failed to produce the desired effect. As the great invasion fleet carrying some 160,000 troops steamed toward its destination, a mistral—a cold north wind that blows into the Mediterranean—struck the armada with gale-force fury. The winds scattered airborne and glider troops across the Sicilian countryside and whipped the seas to a frenzy, dousing shipborne troops and disrupting their landings on July 10.

Despite conditions that almost forced General Eisenhower to delay the invasion, the Allies put a formidable force ashore on D day before daylight and caught the beach defenders off guard. Three of Patton's infantry divisions—the Third, First, and Forty-Fifth—poured ashore at Licata, Gela, and Scoglitti, respectively, along a 50-mile coastal front. Patton held an infantry regiment of the First Division and the Second Armored Division in "floating reserve." Montgomery's Thirtieth and Thirteenth Corps landed on the island's southeast corner. The Eighth Army's 100-mile coastal front stretched from Pozallo on the southwest shore to Avola on the eastern shore.

By the end of the first day, all of the beachheads had been established ashore, and the buildup of some 14,000 vehicles, 600 tanks, 1,800 artillery pieces, and enormous stacks of provisions and munitions was piling up on the beaches. Although Allen's Big Red One division met strong resistance at Gela, corps commander Bradley, now a lieutenant general, counted his blessings later. "All our forces got ashore with negligible casualties and were displaying remarkable aggressiveness."[97]

Heavy seas delayed Patton's arrival on shore until the next morning. By instinct or pure chance, he motored to Gela just in time to help repulse an attack by Axis tanks. He helped a mortar party lay in their 4.2-mm tubes and generally shouted encouragement to all within earshot. With the situation stabilized, he returned to the beach and immediately came under attack by 14 German bombers. He kept his calm and walked about the beach for all his men to see him and draw confidence from his apparent indifference to the danger from above. GSP returned to his HQ on the naval flagship *Monrovia* that night and penned a letter to Beatrice: "This is the first day in this campaign that I think I earned my pay. I am well satisfied with my command today."[98] But Patton was not satisfied with the support role assigned to his army.

After his army established secure lodgments in Sicily, Patton flew to Alexander's headquarters in Tunis to confront him. "General," he said, "I am here to ask you to take the wraps off me and change my orders to read, 'The Seventh Army will drive rapidly to the northwest and north and capture Palermo.'"[99] Alexander, shocked by Patton's passion, granted his request. Patton returned to Sicily and launched a lightning campaign.

Patton's experience in Sicily was characterized by several public relations disasters for the United States. First, Patton refused to pursue prosecution of two American soldiers accused of killing enemy prisoners. The general then went on to visit several field hospitals, where he slapped and insulted wounded American soldiers who he believed were cowards.

While Montgomery's army drove toward Messina in the east, Patton split his forces into two columns. He formed a provisional (temporary) corps under Major General Geoffrey Keyes consisting of the Second Armored, Third Infantry, and Eighty-Second Airborne Divisions and sent them racing west along the coast. And under the direction of Bradley's Second Corps HQ, he sent the First and Forty-Fifth Infantry Divisions pushing straight north. On D day plus 11, Bradley's corps sliced the island in two, and Keyes's corps clattered into Palermo.

"As we approached," Patton wrote later, "the hills on each side were burning. We then started down a long road cut out of the side of a cliff which went through an almost continuous village. The street was full of people shouting, 'Down with Mussolini,' and 'Long live America.'"[100] Keyes had covered 100 miles and cleared the western half of the island in four days. Patton and his subordinate commanders had displayed their talents at modern mobile warfare to the world. But two unfortunate events marred Patton's success.

In two separate incidents near the airfield at Biscari, east of Gela, a sergeant and a captain of the Forty-Fifth Division shot and killed 76 Axis prisoners of war. When informed of the shootings, Patton dismissed the report as a probable exaggeration. He instructed Bradley to tell "the officer responsible for the shootings to certify that the dead men were snipers or had attempted to escape or something."[101] Bradley refused and the two shooters stood trial for murder. Bradley's refusal marked the beginning of a rift in his relationship with Patton.

The sergeant was convicted and sentenced to life imprisonment, but his sentence was later commuted; the captain was acquitted and killed in action soon afterward. The army inspector general grilled Patton on his possible culpability for the incident but soon dropped the investigation. But a few days later, Patton himself committed two imprudent acts that almost ended his career.

While visiting a field hospital, Patton came upon a soldier with no outward signs of injury and asked, "What's the matter with you?"[102]

The soldier replied, "I guess I can't take it, Sir."[103]

Patton flew into a rage, slapped the soldier across the face, and called him a coward and a disgrace. A subsequent investigation revealed that the soldier was running a high fever and suffering from malaria and dysentery.

A week later, in another hospital, Patton approached a soldier suffering from shell shock (now diagnosed as a post-traumatic stress disorder caused by a combat experience). When GSP asked about his condition, the solder replied, "It's my nerves."[104] This time, Patton went virtually berserk.

"Your nerves, hell! You are just a goddamned coward!" Patton shouted, drawing his ivory-handled revolver. "You ought to be shot. In fact I ought to shoot you myself right now, goddamn you!"[105] The soldier started weeping. Patton struck him in the face. Only the intervention of the hospital's commander prevented the untoward incident from escalating further. And only the forbearance of General Eisenhower—who recognized the need for Patton's generalship in the days ahead—restrained him from relieving Patton and sending him home in disgrace. Instead, Ike ordered Patton to make public apologies to all concerned.

As Keyes secured Palermo, Bradley arrived on the northern shore of Sicily, but fierce German resistance from the heights of Mt. Etna had stalled Montgomery at Catania in the east. Patton—whom the press had begun to call "Old Blood and Guts"—now saw a chance for the Americans to beat the British to Messina. He pressured his subordinates to keep advancing as quickly as possible.

In August 1943, Allied forces at last reached their objective of capturing the Italian city of Messina. Less than a month earlier, Italy's Fascist Grand Council had voted to depose Italian dictator Benito Mussolini.

"This is a horse race in which the prestige of the U.S. Army is at stake," he urged. "We must take Messina before the British."[106] And they did.

On August 17, 1943, the first American patrols entered Messina, only hours ahead of advance British elements. But skillful delaying tactics of the enemy had enabled the evacuation of some 40,000 German and 60,000 Italian troops across the narrow Strait of Messina to the Italian mainland. Nevertheless, the Allies had achieved another impressive victory. Axis casualties in the 38-day campaign totaled 167,000; Allied losses were 31,158, including 11,923 Americans. And an added bonus had come on July 24 during the fighting for Sicily, when the Fascist Grand Council met in Rome and deposed Italian dictator Benito Mussolini.

On August 23, Patton issued General Order Number 18 to the soldiers of the U.S. Seventh Army (which had been officially activated at sea while en route to Sicily). The order began, "Born at sea, baptized in blood, and crowned with victory, in the course of thirty-eight days of incessant battle and unceasing labor, you have added a glorious chapter to the history of war."[107] It went on to applaud their accomplishments and ended with, "Your fame shall never die."[108]

Nor would his own, some might say, for he had again demonstrated his mastery of modern mobile warfare on the battlefield. It was a satisfying end to a summer in Sicily.

Glory Days

After Sicily, Patton suffered through several months of disuse until summoned to England, ostensibly to command the nonexistent First U.S. Army Group (FUSAG). In reality, Eisenhower, now the supreme commander of Allied forces in Europe, gave Patton command of the U.S. Third Army. The phantom army was part of an enormous deception known as Operation Fortitude.

The Germans had long been aware that the Allies were assembling in England for an invasion of Europe. But they did not know where or when. The Allies embarked on an elaborate effort to deceive the Germans into believing that the inevitable Allied landings would come across the narrowest part of the

The coordination of the D day invasion was complex and involved Allied forces from the United States, England, and Canada. Patton's role was twofold: First, train and prepare the U.S. Third Army for the invasion, and second, deceive German intelligence about the time and place of the Allied assault with the creation of a fictitious decoy army. Here, Patton (left) confers with U.S. General Omar Bradley and British General Bernard Montgomery.

English Channel, from Dover to the Pas de Calais. The deception formed a part of Operation OVERLORD—the Allied code name for the invasion of Western Europe. It included establishing a dummy headquarters and fake army camps, broadcasting false radio traffic, and even altering Allied bombing patterns in Europe. Allied strategists selected Patton to lead the fictitious First U.S. Army because he was the American general most feared by the Germans.

Patton arrived in London on January 26, 1944, to undertake his dual function. His first concern was to mold the real Third Army in the image of all his other fighting units, and he began, as always, with dress and discipline. In a letter home, a newly arrived staff officer recorded one of GSP's first speeches to his full staff. With his riding crop in hand and his white bull terrier, Willie, at his side, Patton said:

> I can assure you that the Third United States Army will be the greatest army in American history. We shall be in Berlin ahead of every one. To gain that end we must have perfect discipline. I shall drive you until hell won't have it.[109]

The staff officer ended his letter, concluding, "Here was a man for whom you *would* go to hell and back."[110]

The OVERLORD plan called for Montgomery to command the Allied ground forces on the continent until Ike's arrival after the initial Normandy landings. After airborne and glider landings, the U.S. First Army under Bradley was to land on two beaches, and the British Second and the Canadian First Armies were to come ashore on three. D day was set for June 4, 1944, but because of bad weather conditions it was later changed to June 6. Once ashore, the British Second Army was to capture Caen and press on to the Falaise plain to make room on the beaches for the Canadian First Army. Bradley's First Army would in the meantime seize Cherbourg and drive to Avranches. Patton's Third Army was to join the battle there—at the entrance to Brittany—to clear the province of Germans.

As history has grandly recorded, Operation FORTITUDE worked to perfection. The mammoth ploy kept the bulk of German defenders in Western Europe, concentrated in the Pas de Calais area and away from the real invasion sites in Normandy. Beginning with the airdrops shortly after midnight on June 6, 1944, the Allied landings were carried out successfully.

At noon on August 1—six days after the start of the American breakout of Normandy at Avranches—Patton's Third Army became operational as part of General Bradley's newly created Twelfth Army Group. It contained four corps (the Third, Fifth, Twelfth, and Twentieth) comprised of 6 armored and 12 infantry divisions. In a letter to Beatrice a few days later, Patton wrote: "The waiting was pretty bad . . . but now we are in the biggest battle I have ever fought and it is going fine except at one town [St.-Malo] we have failed to take. . . . I am going there in a minute to kick some ones ass."[111]

In less than a week, Patton liberated the entire interior of the province of Brittany. But his lightning campaign in Brittany was not without critics. Historian Caleb Carr notes that "the Third Army's wild rampage through Brittany obscured one central fact—west was precisely the *wrong* direction."[112] Berlin and most of the German army, of course, lay to the east. But Patton's supporters point out that had he, rather than Bradley, been in command of the U.S. Twelfth Army Group at the time, the Third Army might have turned eastward far sooner. Such are the nagging controversies of retrospective analysis.

After his Third Army armor (mechanized units) had cleared Brittany of Germans (except for a few port cities left isolated and under siege), Patton turned his armor south to the Loire River and pointed eastward. His infantry curved left toward Le Mans. Then the Germans suddenly counter-attacked at Mortain, east of Avranches.

General Bradley sent mobile columns of both GSP's Third Army and the U.S. First Army—now under Lieutenant General Courtney H. Hodges—wheeling northward toward Argentan, near Falaise. He coordinated the maneuver with General Montgomery, who sent his forces driving south. The Allied movement snared the counterattacking Germans in a giant pocket. But the late arrival of the British forces resulted in a 15-mile opening in the pocket between Argentan and Falaise. The opening—later known as the Falaise Gap—allowed many Germans to escape. Even so, the Allies still captured or killed some 60,000 Germans and seized huge masses of German tanks, guns, and matériel in the pocket.

Even the Germans who escaped through the gap suffered a terrible pounding from Allied airpower. "Forty-eight hours after the closing of the gap," wrote Eisenhower, "I was conducted through it on foot, to encounter scenes that could be described only by Dante [as in his vision of Hell in *The Divine Comedy*]. It was literally possible to walk for hundreds of yards at a time, stepping on nothing but dead and decaying human flesh."[113]

While the First Army mopped up at Argentan, Patton's Third Army roared off again toward the Seine River with two objectives in mind: first, to prevent the retreating Germans from using the river as a new line of defense; and second, to trap the Germans who had escaped at Falaise in a wider envelopment. He accomplished both aims, crossing the Seine on August 19. In two weeks of fighting, the Germans had lost large segments of two field armies. And across the Seine, many great roads led to the heart of Germany.

In the meantime, Lieutenant General Alexander Patch's Seventh Army landed in southern France on August 15

A two-pronged attack by U.S. and British armored divisions at Falaise, France, ensnared thousands of counterattacking German troops. In an area known as the "Falaise pocket," more than 60,000 German soldiers were killed, and many others taken prisoner. Here, we see some of the POWs captured by Allied troops.

and advanced rapidly to Dijon, where it hooked up with Patton's Third Army on September 11. The Seventh Army later formed a part of the U.S. Sixth Army Group under Lieutenant General Jacob L. Devers.

By the time Patton reached the Seine, he had become a real-life living legend whose name was emblazoned in newspaper headlines and touted in radio broadcasts. One broadcaster said of him: "Striding across a battlefield, two 45-caliber Colt revolvers strapped to his hips, or riding his tanks, with his head poking out, cased in a huge helmet, his eyes glare, and he roars encouragement, orders, advice, and oaths all at once."[114] History books abound with wild tales about the pistol-packing general—some true, some not—but all evoking the image of a man mightier than the myths surrounding him.

On August 21, GSP noted in his diary: "We have, at this time, the greatest chance to win the war ever presented. If they will let me move on with three corps, two up and one back, on the line of Metz-Nancy-Epinal, we can be in Germany in ten days." [115] But fate and Montgomery would have none of it.

In September 1944, Patton entertained visions of leading his Third Army—and the rest of the Allied forces—across the Rhine. All he needed, he asserted, was sufficient fuel and ammunition. He wanted to pursue the uprooted Germans before they could regroup. But the now Field Marshal Montgomery cherished a similar notion and diverted supplies from the Third Army for his own use, and Patton's drive stalled. His Third Army was literally out of gas.

The advance of Allied forces slowed to a crawl. Heavy rains and record cold added to their difficulties. Patton's Third Army reached the West Wall—Germany's fortified western frontier along the Saar River northeast of Metz— in mid-December. The U.S. First and Ninth Armies then stood at the Roer River east of Aachen, 23 miles inside Germany. Suddenly, the Germans turned on the slowly advancing Allies and counterattacked in what the Germans later termed the Ardennes Offensive. The rest of the world knows it better as the Battle of the Bulge (December 16, 1944–January 28, 1945).

The German-induced "bulge" in the Allied lines eventually reached a depth of 60 miles and measured 40 miles at its base. Four days into the battle, the U.S. 101st Airborne Division found itself surrounded and battling to survive at Bastogne in southeast Belgium. On December 22 at 11:30 A.M., the Germans demanded the surrender of the Americans. Brigadier General Anthony C. McAuliffe, commander of the 101st Airborne Division, answered in a word: "Nuts!" [116] McAuliffe and his troopers held out against a merciless German assault for the next five days.

In a meeting with Eisenhower, Patton volunteered to stop at the West Wall and rush to the aid of McAuliffe; Ike said go. Patton wheeled his army 90 degrees and dashed northward to the relief of the entrapped division. This counterthrust of Patton's Third Army arguably constitutes his most remarkable military feat because of the complexity of the maneuver and the speed with which he accomplished it.

On the afternoon of December 26, advance units of Patton's Fourth Armored Division approached to within four miles of Bastogne. Colonel Creighton W. Abrams, commander of the Thirty-Seventh Tank Battalion, radioed his headquarters to ask if Patton would authorize a direct attack on the town. "I sure as hell will!"[117] Patton replied.

At 3:00 P.M., Abrams, standing up in the turret of his 40-ton Sherman tank, stuffed a cigar in his mouth and said, "We're going in to those people now. Let 'er roll!"[118] And they rolled. Smashing Germans in their path, Patton's tankers, followed by half-tracks filled with infantry, lifted the siege of Bastogne.

Within a week, Patton had moved almost a quarter-million men and thousands of tanks and trucks between 50 and 70 miles over treacherous wintry roads to accomplish an all-but-impossible mission. Afterward in a letter to Beatrice, he humbly declared, "The relief of Bastogne is the most brilliant operation we have thus far performed and is in my opinion the outstanding achievement of the war. Now the enemy must dance to our tune, not we to his."[119] Hitler's last desperate offensive in the Ardennes ended on January 28, 1945, and the Western Allies, in concert with the opening of a new Soviet offensive, pressed on toward the Rhine River and the German heartland.

The Germans now stood little chance of holding back the Allies west of the Rhine. Field Marshal K.R. Gerd

With the U.S. 101st Airborne Division under siege at Bastogne, Belgium, Patton and his tanks rushed nearly 70 miles north to their aid. On the day after Christmas, 1944, Patton's tanks and infantry rolled through German lines and ended the siege. Here we see Generals Bradley, Eisenhower, and Patton following the victory.

von Rundstedt, top German field commander, wanted to conserve his remaining strength for a defense of the river, but Hitler ordered no retreat. Thus, Rundstedt lost some 250,000 troops defending strong points along the Roer River and the West Wall—Germany's fortified western frontier—that might have been used to better advantage east of the Rhine.

Keeping the pressure on the fleeing Germans, Patton and his Third Army crossed the Rhine at Mainz and Oppenheim on March 22, 1945, a day ahead of the main crossing by Montgomery's forces farther north. The next day, he issued General Order Number 70 to his Third Army personnel. It said, in part:

> In the period from January 29 to March 22, 1945, you have wrested 6,484 square miles of territory from the enemy. You have taken 3,072 cities, towns, and villages . . .
>
> You have captured 140,112 enemy soldiers and have killed or wounded an additional 99,000, thereby eliminating practically all of the German Seventh and First Armies. History records no greater achievement in so limited a time. . . .
>
> Please accept my heartfelt admiration and thanks for what you have done, and remember that your assault crossing over the Rhine . . . assures you of even greater glory to come.[120]

When the final figures of the Third Army's achievements were tallied, the numbers of German casualties far exceeded those cited in the foregoing general order. Early in April, Patton's men had captured 400,000 prisoners, a total that exceeded one million by war's end.

Patton received his fourth star in April. He learned of his promotion through an item in the *Stars and Stripes,* a newspaper published by and for American soldiers. He received the news without elation: He had expected it. Besides, as he had written to Bea earlier, "I am having so much fun fighting that I don't care what the rank is."[121] But there was little more than a month's fighting left to be done.

Patton wrote to Beatrice, "The war looks over to me. We seem to be able to go anywhere."[122] And that is what the

Allies did. Their armies fanned out from the Rhine and advanced all along the line with massive columns of armor and motorized infantry.

In April, the Third Army swept across southern Germany, captured Nuremberg, crossed the Danube, and bore down on the border of Czechoslovakia. To the north, Montgomery's Twenty-First Army Group secured the Netherlands and headed for the base of the Jutland Peninsula, while the rest of Bradley's Twelfth Army Group encircled the Ruhr moving eastward, taking some 325,000 prisoners and destroying an entire German army group. Southwest of the Third Army, the U.S. Sixth Army Group under Lieutenant General Jacob L. Devers turned southeastward to head off any German attempt to make a last-ditch stand in the Alps of southern Germany and Austria.

In the east, an advance guard of the Soviet Army met an American patrol from the U.S. First Army at Torgau on the Elbe River on April 25, at last joining the West with the East. Hitler committed suicide in Berlin on April 30, and the city fell to the Soviets on May 2. And in the Alps, the U.S. Sixth Army linked up with Lieutenant General Mark W. Clark's Fifth Army on May 4.

On May 5, Patton was preparing to attack Pilsen and move on to capture Prague. But General Eisenhower, not wanting to risk additional American lives on a purely political objective, left the Czech capital to the Soviets. Ike ordered Patton to stop at Pilsen. General Bradley, fearing that Patton might ignore the stated stop line, telephoned him the next day to reaffirm Ike's order. "You hear me, George, goddammit, *halt!*"[123] His words effectively ended the war for Patton. Germany's unconditional surrender on May 7, 1945, made it official.

The god of war had smiled on General George Smith Patton Jr. He had led one of the most successful armies of all time, scribed his name in the book of great generals, and survived the most violent war in history. But he rejoiced not. With the end of the war, as he told Beatrice, "I will be out of a job. . . . I love war and responsibility and excitement. Peace is going to be hell on me."[124]

Patton was right. His glory days ended with the war. All that remained was hell.

Patton's Honor

On May 10, 1945, Patton issued General Order Number 98. He characterized it as "terminating the war." In the order – as published in George Forty's *The Armies of George S. Patton* – he summed up the achievements of the U.S. Third Army this way:

> During the 281 days of incessant and victorious combat, your penetrations have advanced farther in less time than any other army in history. You have fought your way across 24 major rivers and innumerable lesser streams. You have conquered more than 82,000 square miles of territory, including 1,500 cities and towns, and some 12,000 inhabited places. Prior to the termination of active hostilities, you had captured in battle 956,000 enemy soldiers and killed and wounded at least 500,000 others. France, Belgium, Luxembourg, Germany, Austria and Czechoslovakia bear witness of your exploits.

The order went on to pay tribute to all the Allied elements that had supported the Third Army and homage to all the heroic dead and wounded whose sacrifices had made victory possible. Of his own role as Third Army commander, Patton wrote:

> During the course of this war I have received promotion and decorations far above and beyond my individual merit. You have won them: I as your representative wear them. The one honor which is mine and mine alone is that of having commanded such an incomparable group of Americans, the record of whose fortitude, audacity and valor will endure as long as history lasts.

Afterword: Destiny

Patton stayed on in Germany as the first peacetime commander of the Third Army. But the glory was gone. And the personal hell that he had foreseen for himself was set to begin. First, however, he returned to the United States in June for a well-earned leave and a round of personal appearances before throngs of grateful Americans.

Before returning to Europe in July, he turned to his daughters Bee and Ruth Ellen and said, "Well, I guess this is goodbye. I won't be seeing you again."[125] They protested but he stifled their objections. Pausing, he added, "I think I'll see your mother again."[126] He had experienced a premonition of death, and he felt convinced of its validity.

After the war in Europe had ended, Patton stayed on as commander of the Third Army. Though hailed as a hero, he had a premonition of his own death. On a brief return home to the United States on leave, he told his daughters that he probably would not see them again.

Back in Europe, in the new Third Army headquarters at Bad Tolz in Bavaria, he soon found himself burdened with the many administrative duties essential to governing and rehabilitating a broken nation. As the military governor of Bavaria, he quickly ran afoul of Eisenhower's directive to remove and exclude former Nazis from public office. "I had never heard that we fought to de-natzify Germany—live and learn," Patton wrote Beatrice. "What we are doing is to utterly destroy the only semi-modern state in Europe so that Russia can swallow the whole."[127]

Patton believed deeply that the United States would inevitably be forced to fight the Soviet Union. He did not trust either the British or the French as allies. Further, he felt that the Germans—whom he believed had fought honorably against him—would make staunch allies in the coming war against "the Mongols,"[128] as he termed the Soviets. But not if the victors castigated all former Nazis, he believed, and refused to recognize their usefulness in rebuilding Germany.

His views—which he made no secret of—were unpopular at the time. Americans and their allies had fought the war to eliminate immoral regimes. Patton had missed the point, believing that "Germany should not be destroyed but rather rebuilt as a buffer against the real danger, which is Bolshevism [communism] from Russia"[129]—even if it entailed retaining former Nazis in positions of authority.

On September 29, Eisenhower notified Patton of his transfer to head the Fifteenth Army in Bad Nauheim, a "paper army" charged with documenting the lessons of the European campaign. To Bea, Patton confided, "Were it not for the fact that it will be, so far as I am concerned, a kick up stairs, I would like it much better than being a sort of executioner to the best race in Europe."[130] Patton now looked forward to returning home for Christmas. Once back in the United States, he planned either to find a better position for himself or to retire.

On December 9, the day before he was scheduled to leave for home, Patton and his friend and chief of staff Major General Hobart R. "Hap" Gay left Bad Nauheim in Patton's 1939 Model 75 Cadillac to shoot pheasants in Mannheim. On the way to the hunting site, they passed a supply yard that was serving as a collection point for scrapped vehicles. Patton exclaimed, "Look at all the derelict vehicles! How awful war is. Think of the waste."[131] GSP's driver, Private First Class Horace L. Woodring, diverted his eyes for a moment to view the derelicts. His eyes returned to the road a split second later, just as a two-and-a-half ton GMC truck turned left in front of Patton's Cadillac.

"I saw him in time to hit my brakes but not in time to do anything," [132] Woodring said later. Both vehicles were moving slowly, the truck at 10 miles an hour, the Cadillac at 30. The GMC sustained little damage, but its right front bumper smashed the right front side of the Cadillac, demolishing its headlights, radiator, and front fender. Everyone had been shaken, but no one appeared to be badly hurt at first. The impact of the collision, however, had thrown Patton forward into the rail of the open partition separating the front and rear seats and then jerked him backward into Gay's arms.

"It took all the skin from the General's forehead for approximately three inches above his eyebrows and three inches across," Woodring recalled later, "partially scalping him and completely separating his spinal column [between the third and fourth cervical vertebrae]." [133] Part of the damage to his scalp likely resulted from grazing the diamond-shaped light fixture on the roof's interior. His nose was also broken and he was paralyzed from the neck down.

An MP (military police) officer arrived on the scene and Gay directed him to call the medics and an ambulance. While awaiting the ambulance, Patton murmured ruefully, "This is a helluva way to die." [134] The ambulance arrived soon afterward and rushed him to the 130th Station Hospital in Heidelberg, 25 miles away. At 60 years of age, Patton now faced the toughest battle of his life.

Doctors diagnosed the spinal fracture in Patton's neck and affixed two razor-sharp zygomatic hooks to his cheek-bones. The hooks were attached in turn to a ten-pound weight that formed a part of a traction device designed to pull and extend GSP's head and backbone and thereby relieve the pressure on his spine. The army summoned experts in the field of neurosurgery to attend him and flew Beatrice to his side to comfort him.

For a time, Patton's condition seemed to improve enough for the army to consider flying him home, although he remained paralyzed from the neck down. But on December 19, he began to experience difficulty breathing.

On December 21, Patton appeared very drowsy but somewhat improved. At one point that morning, he said to Beatrice, "It's too dark . . . I mean too late."[135] She spent much of the day reading to him, while he drifted in and out of sleep. At 5:15 P.M., while he was sleeping peacefully, she left to have dinner with two attending doctors in the hospital mess across the street. Another doctor summoned her back to her husband's bedside at 6:00 P.M. When she reached his room, she found him dead. Patton had died in his sleep.

R. Glen Spurling, an American neurosurgeon who had flown to Germany with Beatrice, afterward commented that Patton had never voiced a word of complaint. He "died as he had lived—bravely."[136] Army records officially list the cause of Patton's death as "pulmonary edema and congestive heart failure."[137] The final entry in his medical log states starkly: "17:55 hours. Expired."[138] It was the only battle Patton ever lost.

■   ■   ■

Patton lives on in legend as one of America's greatest warriors. He was and remains many things to many people—at alternate times crude and cultured; cruel and compassionate; egotistical and self-effacing; confident on the outside, uncertain of his ability on the inside; a flamboyant, pistol-packing, cursing leader of men as well as a

Despite many brushes with death during battle, it would be a car accident that would finally take Patton's life. The crash between the general's car and a supply truck caused severe spinal injuries and paralysis. Patton died 12 days later at a German hospital in Heidelberg. Here, soldiers transport Patton's coffin through a train station in Luxembourg.

sensitive, scholarly, poetic student of history and the arts. His complex personality seemed always to exhibit two sides in all things, each in total opposition to the other. Yet, somehow his mix of opposing characteristics produced an uncommon genius on the battlefield.

Perhaps the most reliable test of Patton's leadership lies in the opinions of those who served under him and of those who faced him on the battlefield. In the first instance, a young soldier, who was on duty in Heidelberg

This grave marks Patton's final resting place in the American cemetery at Hamm, Luxembourg. He lies beside many of the fallen men who had given their lives in the name of freedom. His widow, Beatrice, said he would have wanted it that way.

when Patton died, wrote to tell his parents that he was "in mourning" for:

> . . . one of the greatest men that ever lived. . . . The rest of the world thinks of him as just another guy with stars on his shoulders. The men who served under him know him as a soldier's leader. I am proud to say that I have served under him in the Third Army.[139]

And in the second instance, a high-ranking German officer who had been captured just before the war ended said:

> General Patton is the most feared general on all fronts. . . . The tactics of General Patton are daring and unpredictable. . . . He is the most modern general and the best commander of armored and infantry troops combined.[140]

Those who served under him and those who fought against him could see through his often crude exterior to the greatness that lay beneath. Patton would have liked that.

Patton lies buried in the American cemetery at Hamm, Luxembourg, at the head of the men of his Third Army who fought—and died fighting—with him in the Ardennes. Beatrice, his true love and devoted companion, approved his gravesite. "I know George would want to lie beside the men of his army who have fallen," [141] she said.

In life and in death, General George Smith Patton Jr. was meant to be at the head of an army. From childhood's hour, it was his destiny.

1885

November 11   George Smith Patton Jr. is born in San Gabriel, California.

1903   Enters Virginia Military Institute.

1904–1909   Attends and graduates from the U.S. Military Academy at West
                 Point, New York; commissioned second lieutenant in the cavalry.

1910

May 26   Marries Beatrice Banning Ayer.

1911

March 11   First daughter, Beatrice Jr., born to Pattons.

1912   Participates in Olympic Games in Stockholm, Sweden.

1915

February 28   Second daughter, Ruth Ellen, born to Pattons.

1916

May 14   Shoot-out with Pancho Villa's henchmen near San Miguelito,
                 Mexico.

1918

September 12–16 St.-Mihiel offensive.

September 26   Patton is wounded during the Meuse-Argonne offensive.

November 11   Armistice; World War I ends.

1923

December 24   Only son, George IV, born to the Pattons.

1939

September 1   Hitler's armies invade Poland; World War II begins.

1940

October 2   Promoted to brigadier general.

1941

April 1   Promoted to major general.

December 7   Japanese attack U.S. military installations at Pearl Harbor, Hawaii,
                 and in the Philippines; America enters World War II.

1942

November 8–11   TORCH landings in French North Africa; commands Western
                 Task Force.

1943

February 14–22	Battle of Kasserine Pass.
March 17–31	Battle of El Guettar; commands U.S. Second Corps.
May 12	Promoted to lieutenant general.
July 10–August 17	Battle for Sicily; commands U.S. Seventh Army.

1944

June 6	Invasion of Normandy.
August 1	U.S. Third Army becomes operational with Patton in command.
December 16	Battle of the Bulge begins.

1945

January 28	Battle of the Bulge ends.
April 14	Promoted to general.
May 8	War ends in Europe.
October 6	Relieved of command of Third Army; assigned as commanding general of Fifteenth Army.
December 9	Involved in automobile accident near Mannheim; hospitalized in Heidelberg.
December 21	General George S. Patton Jr. dies.
December 24	Interred at Luxembourg.

CHAPTER 1

1. Quoted in Carlo D'Este, *Patton: A Genius for War*. New York: HarperCollins, 1995, p. 249.
2. Quoted in Edward M. Coffman, *The War to End All Wars: The American Military Experience in World War I*. Lexington, KY: University Press of Kentucky, 1998, p. 304.
3. Quoted in Martin Blumenson, *The Patton Papers 1885–1940*. New York: Da Capo, 1998, p. 607.
4. Ibid., p. 604.
5. Ibid.
6. Quoted in D'Este, *Patton*, p. 249.
7. Quoted in Blumenson, *The Patton Papers 1885–1940*, p. 609.
8. Quoted in D'Este, *Patton*, p. 254.
9. Ibid., p. 255.
10. Ibid.
11. Ibid., p. 257.
12. Quoted in Martin Blumenson, *Patton: The Man behind the Legend, 1885–1945*. New York: William Morrow, 1985, p. 113.
13. Quoted in John S. D. Eisenhower with Joanne T. Eisenhower, *Yanks: The Epic Story of the American Army in World War I*. New York: Free Press, 2001, p. 218.
14. Ibid.
15. Quoted in John Toland, *No Man's Land: 1918, The Last Year of the Great War*. New York: Ballantine Books, 1980, p. 332.
16. Ibid.
17. Ibid.
18. Quoted in D'Este, *Patton*, p. 259.
19. Quoted in Blumenson, *Patton*, p. 114.
20. Ibid., p. 115.

CHAPTER 2

21. Quoted in Blumenson, *Patton*, p. 20.
22. Quoted in D'Este, *Patton*, p. 12.
23. Quoted in Blumenson, *Patton*, p. 24.
24. Ibid.
25. Quoted in D'Este, *Patton*, p. 29.
26. Blumenson, *Patton*, pp. 24–25.
27. Quoted in D'Este, *Patton*, p. 39.
28. Ibid.
29. Ibid.
30. Quoted in George Forty, *The Armies of George S. Patton*. London: Arms and Armour, 1996, p. 16.
31. Quoted in D'Este, *Patton*, p. 33.
32. Ibid., p. 51.
33. Ibid., p. 31.
34. Ibid., p. 69.

CHAPTER 3

35. Quoted in Blumenson, *The Patton Papers 1885–1940*, p. 185.
36. Quoted in Forty, *The Armies of George S. Patton*, p. 17.
37. Ibid.
38. Quoted in Blumenson, *Patton*, p. 64.
39. Quoted in Forty, *The Armies of George S. Patton*, p. 17.
40. Ibid.
41. Quoted in Blumenson, *Patton*, p. 74.
42. Ibid., p. 92.
43. Quoted in D'Este, *Patton*, p. 177.
44. Ibid.

CHAPTER 4

45. Quoted in Forty, *The Armies of George S. Patton*, p. 19.
46. Forty, *The Armies of George S. Patton*, p. 20.
47. Quoted in Ibid., p. 24.
48. Quoted in D'Este, *Patton*, pp. 234–35.
49. Quoted in Blumenson, *Patton*, p. 110.
50. Ibid.
51. Quoted in D'Este, *Patton*, p. 246.
52. Ibid., p. 243.
53. Ibid., p. 246.
54. Ibid., pp. 246–47.

CHAPTER 5

55. Quoted in Blumenson, *Patton*, p. 120.
56. Ibid.
57. Ibid., p. 127.
58. Quoted in D'Este, *Patton*, p. 331.
59. Ibid., p. 362.
60. Ibid.
61. Ibid., p. 359.
62. Quoted in Blumenson, *The Patton Papers 1885–1940*, p. 929.
63. Quoted in D'Este, *Patton*, p. 368.
64. Quoted in Blumenson, *The Patton Papers 1885–1940*, p. 931.
65. Quoted in Forty, *The Armies of George S. Patton*, p. 28.

CHAPTER 6

66. Quoted in Martin Blumenson, *The Patton Papers 1940–1945*. New York: Da Capo, 1974, p. 13.
67. Ibid., p. 14.
68. Quoted in Blumenson, *Patton*, p. 150.
69. Ibid., p. 152.
70. Quoted in Blumenson, *The Patton Papers 1940–1945*, p. 44.
71. Quoted in Blumenson, *Patton*, p. 161.
72. Ibid., p. 165.
73. Quoted in D'Este, *Patton*, p. 427.
74. Quoted in Forty, *The Armies of George S. Patton*, p. 39.

CHAPTER 7

75. George S. Patton Jr., *War As I Knew It*. Boston: Houghton Mifflin, 1995, p. 5.
76. Quoted in Blumenson, *The Patton Papers 1940–1945*, p. 102.
77. Quoted in D'Este, *Patton*, p. 437.
78. Quoted in Blumenson, *Patton*, p. 170.
79. Quoted in Blumenson, *The Patton Papers 1940–1945*, p. 110.
80. Quoted in Sidney C. Moody Jr. and the Associated Press, *War in Europe*. Novato, CA: Presidio Press, 1993, p. 83.
81. Quoted in Blumenson, *Patton*, p. 183.
82. Quoted in D'Este, *Patton*, p. 471.
83. Ibid., p. 476.
84. Ibid.
85. Quoted in Blumenson, *The Patton Papers 1940–1945*, p. 206.
86. Ibid.
87. Ibid., p. 207.
88. Quoted in D'Este, *Patton*, p. 481.
89. Ibid.
90. Quoted in Omar N. Bradley and Clay Blair, *A General's Life: An Autobiography by General of the Army Omar N. Bradley and Clay Blair*. New York: Simon & Schuster, 1983, p. 148.
91. Quoted in Blumenson, *The Patton Papers 1940–1945*, p. 213.
92. Ibid.
93. Quoted in Forty, *The Armies of George S. Patton*, p. 47.

CHAPTER 8

94. Quoted in Blumenson, *The Patton Papers 1940–1945*, p. 223.
95. Quoted in Blumenson, *Patton*, p. 189.
96. Quoted in Forty, *The Armies of George S. Patton*, pp. 50–51.
97. Bradley and Blair, *A General's Life*, p. 181.
98. Quoted in Blumenson, *The Patton Papers 1940–1945*, p. 280.
99. Quoted in Editors of Time-Life Books, *WW II: The Time-Life History of World War II*. New York: Barnes & Noble, 1995, p. 227.
100. Quoted in Robert Leckie, *The Wars of America*. Vol. 2: *From 1900 to 1992*. New York: HarperCollins, 1992, p. 766.
101. Quoted in C. B. Dear and M. R. D. Foot, eds. *The Oxford Companion to World War II*. New York: Oxford University Press, 1995, p. 132.
102. Quoted in Editors of Time-Life Books, *WW II*, p. 227.
103. Ibid.
104. Ibid.
105. Ibid.
106. Quoted in Blumenson, *Patton*, p. 202.
107. Patton, *War As I Knew It*, p. 64.
108. Ibid.

CHAPTER 9

109. Quoted in D'Este, *Patton*, p. 573.
110. Ibid.
111. Quoted in Blumenson, *The Patton Papers 1940–1945*, p. 501.
112. Quoted in D'Este, *Patton*, p. 634.
113. Quoted in Leckie, *The Wars of America*, p. 804.
114. Quoted in Blumenson, *The Patton Papers 1940–1945*, p. 524.
115. Ibid., p. 523.
116. Quoted in John Toland, *Battle: The Story of the Bulge*. New York: Random House, 1959, p. 193.
117. Ibid., p. 263.
118. Ibid.
119. Quoted in Blumenson, *Patton*, pp. 251–52.
120. Quoted in Blumenson, *The Patton Papers 1940–1945*, pp. 660–61.
121. Ibid., p. 656.
122. Ibid., p. 677.
123. Quoted in Carlo D'Este, *Eisenhower: A Soldier's Life*. New York: Henry Holt, 2002, p. 699.
124. Quoted in Blumenson, *The Patton Papers 1940–1945*, p. 695.

CHAPTER 10

125. Quoted in D'Este, *Patton*, p. 750.
126. Ibid.
127. Quoted in Blumenson, *The Patton Papers 1940–1945*, p. 746.
128. Quoted in Blumenson, *Patton*, p. 287.
129. Quoted in Blumenson, *The Patton Papers 1940–1945*, p. 784.
130. Ibid., p. 786.
131. Quoted in D'Este, *Patton*, p. 785.
132. Quoted in Forty, *The Armies of George S. Patton*, p. 251.
133. Quoted in D'Este, *Patton*, p. 786.
134. Ibid., p. 785.
135. Ibid., p. 795.
136. Quoted in Blumenson, *Patton*, p. 293.
137. Quoted in D'Este, *Patton*, p. 796.
138. Ibid.
139. Quoted in Blumenson, *Patton*, p. 296.
140. Ibid.
141. Quoted in D'Este, *Patton*, p. 798.

Ambrose, Stephen E., and C. L. Sulzberger. *American Heritage New History of World War II*. New York: Viking, 1997.

Astor, Gerald. *A Blood-Dimmed Tide: The Battle of the Bulge by the Men Who Fought It*. New York: Bantam Doubleday Dell, 1992.

Barnett, Correlli, ed. *Hitler's Generals*. New York: Quill/William Morrow, 1989.

Blumenson, Martin. *The Patton Papers 1885–1940*. New York: Da Capo, 1998.

———. *The Patton Papers 1940–1945*. New York: Da Capo, 1974.

———. *Patton: The Man behind the Legend, 1885–1945*. New York: William Morrow, 1985.

Bradley, Omar N., and Clay Blair. *A General's Life: An Autobiography by General of the Army Omar N. Bradley and Clay Blair*. New York: Simon & Schuster, 1983.

Coffman, Edward M. *The War to End All Wars: The American Military Experience in World War I*. Lexington, KY: University Press of Kentucky, 1998.

Dear, C.B., and M.R.D. Foot, eds. *The Oxford Companion to World War II*. New York: Oxford University Press, 1995.

D'Este, Carlo. *Eisenhower: A Soldier's Life*. New York: Henry Holt, 2002.

———. *Patton: A Genius for War*. New York: HarperCollins, 1995.

Dupuy, Ernest, and Trevor Dupuy. *The Encyclopedia of Military History: From 3500 B.C. to the Present*. Rev. ed. New York: Harper & Row, 1986.

Editors of Time-Life Books. *WW II: The Time-Life History of World War II*. New York: Barnes & Noble, 1995.

Eisenhower, Dwight D. *Crusade in Europe*. Baltimore, MD: Johns Hopkins University Press, 1997.

Eisenhower, John S.D., with Joanne T. Eisenhower. *Yanks: The Epic Story of the American Army in World War I*. New York: Free Press, 2001.

Essame, H. *Patton as Military Commander*. Military Commander series. Conshohocken, PA: Combined Publishing, 1998.

Forty, George. *The Armies of George S. Patton*. London: Arms and Armour, 1996.

Hanson, Victor Davis. *The Soul of Battle: From Ancient Times to the Present Day, How Three Great Liberators Vanquished Tyranny*. New York: Free Press, 1999.

Leckie, Robert. *The Wars of America*. Vol. 2: *From 1900 to 1992*. New York: Harper-Collins, 1992.

MacDonald, Charles B. *The Mighty Endeavor: The American War in Europe*. New York: Da Capo Press, 1992.

Mansoor, Peter R. *The GI Offensive in Europe: The Triumph of American Infantry Divisions, 1941–1945*. Lawrence, KS: University Press of Kansas, 1999.

Moody, Jr., Sidney C., and the Associated Press. *War in Europe*. Novato, CA: Presidio Press, 1993.

Morison, Samuel Eliot. *The Invasion of France and Germany, 1944–1945*. Vol. 11 of *History of United States Naval Operations in World War II*. Edison, NJ: Castle Books, 2001.

————. *Sicily Salerno Anzio, January 1943–June 1944*. Vol. 9 of *History of United States Naval Operations in World War II*. Boston: Little, Brown, 1954.

Patton, George S., Jr. *War As I Knew It*. Boston: Houghton Mifflin, 1995.

Polmar, Norman, and Thomas B. Allen, eds. *World War II: The Encyclopedia of the War Years 1941–1945*. New York: Random House, 1996.

Reader's Digest Association. *Reader's Digest Illustrated Story of World War II*. Pleasantville, NY: Reader's Digest Association, 1978.

Rice, Earle, Jr. *Strategic Battles in Europe*. American War Library Series. San Diego, CA: Lucent Books, 2000.

Rolf, David. *The Bloody Road to Tunis: Destruction of the Axis Forces in North Africa, November 1942–May 1943*. Mechanicsburg, PA: Stackpole Books, 2001.

Toland, John. *No Man's Land: 1918, The Last Year of the Great War*. New York: Ballantine Books, 1980.

————. *Battle: The Story of the Bulge*. New York: Random House, 1959.

Whiting, Charles. *Ghost Front: The Ardennes before the Battle of the Bulge*. New York: Da Capo, 2002.

————. *West Wall: The Battle for Hitler's Siegfried Line*. Kent, UK: Spellmount, 1999.

Wilson, Theodore A., ed. *D-Day 1944*. Lawrence, KS: University Press of Kansas, 1994.

Ambrose, Stephen E. *Americans at War*. Jackson, MS: University Press of Mississippi, 1997.

Badsey, Stephen. *Normandy 1944: Allied Landings and Breakout*. Campaign Series. General Editor David G. Chandler. Oxford, UK: Osprey Publishing, 1999.

Black, Robert W. *Rangers in World War II*. New York: Ballantine Books, 1992.

Brokaw, Tom. *The Greatest Generation*. New York: Random House, 1998.

Chandler, David G. *Battles and Battle Scenes of World War Two*. New York: Macmillan, 1989.

Chandler, David G., Colin McIntyre, and Michael C. Tagg. *Chronicles of World War II*. Godalming, UK: Bramley Books, 1997.

Chant, Christopher, ed. *Warfare and the Third Reich: The Rise and Fall of Hitler's Armed Forces*. New York: Smithmark, 1996.

Christman, Calvin L., ed. *America at War: An Anthology of Articles from MHQ: The Quarterly Journal of Military History*. Annapolis, MD: Naval Institute Press, 1995.

Congdon, Don. *Combat World War II Europe: Unforgettable Eyewitness Accounts of the Momentous Military Struggles of World War II*. New York: Galahad Books, 1996.

Doubler, Michael D. *Closing with the Enemy: How GIs Fought the War in Europe, 1944–1945*. Lawrence, KS: University Press of Kansas, 1994.

Dunnigan, James F., and Albert A. Nofi. *Dirty Little Secrets of World War II: Military Information No One Told You about the Greatest, Most Terrible War in History*. New York: William Morrow, 1994.

Flower, Desmond, and James Reeves, eds. *The War, 1939–1945: A Documentary History*. New York: Da Capo Press, 1997.

Gilbert, Martin. *The Second World War: A Complete History*. New York: Henry Holt, 1989.

Halliwell, Sarah, and Tim Cooke, eds. *Eyewitness War*. South Woodham Ferrers, UK: Publishing Corporation UK Ltd., 1995.

Hynes, Samuel. *The Soldiers' Tale: Bearing Witness to Modern War*. New York: Viking, 1997.

Jablonski, Edward. *A Pictorial History of the World War II Years*. New York: Wings Books, 1995.

Kilvert-Jones, Tim. *Omaha Beach: V Corps' Battle for the Normandy Beachhead*. Battleground Europe Series. Barnsley, UK: Leo Cooper/Pen & Sword Books, 1999.

Library of America. *Reporting World War II, Part Two: American Journalism 1944–1946*. New York: Library Classics of the United States, 1995.

Linderman, Gerald F. *The World within War: America's Combat Experience in World War II*. New York: Free Press, 1997.

McCombs, Don, and Fred L. Worth. *World War II: 4,139 Strange and Fascinating Facts*. New York: Wings Books, 1996.

McManus, John C. *The Deadly Brotherhood: The American Combat Soldier in World War II*. Novato, CA: Presidio Press, 1998.

Messenger, Charles. *Sepp Dietrich: Hitler's Gladiator; the Life and Times of Oberstgruppen-führer and Panzergeneral-Oberst der Waffen-SS Dietrich*. London: Brassey's, 1988.

Miller, David. *Great Battles of World War II: Major Operations That Affected the Course of the War*. New York: Crescent Books, 1998.

Miller, Robert A. *August 1944: The Campaign for France*. Novato, CA: Presidio Press, 1988.

Murphy, Edward F. *Heroes of World War II*. Novato, CA: Presidio Press, 1990.

O'Neill, William L. *A Democracy at War: America's Fight at Home and Abroad in World War II*. New York: Free Press, 1993.

Shilleto, Carl. *Utah Beach, St Mère Église*. Battleground Europe Series. Barnsley, UK: Leo Cooper/Pen & Sword Books, 2001.

Sulzberger, C. L. *World War II*. New York: American Heritage, 1985.

Taylor, A. J. P. *The Second World War and Its Aftermath*. London: Folio Society, 1998.

Terkel, Studs. *"The Good War": An Oral History of World War II*. New York: New Press, 1990.

page:

EARLE RICE JR. is a former senior design engineer and technical writer in the aerospace industry. After serving nine years with the U.S. Marine Corps, he attended San Jose City College and Foothill College on the San Francisco Peninsula. He has devoted full time to his writing since 1993 and has written more than forty books for young adults. Earle is a member of the Society of Children's Book Writers and Illustrators; the League of World War I Aviation Historians and its UK-based sister organization, Cross & Cockade International; the United States Naval Institute; and the Air Force Association.

CASPAR W. WEINBERGER was the fifteenth secretary of defense, serving under President Ronald Reagan from 1981 to 1987. Born in California in 1917, he fought in the Pacific during World War II then went on to pursue a law career. He became an active member of the California Republican Party and was named the party's chairman in 1962. Over the next decade, Weinberger held several federal government offices, including chairman of the Federal Trade Commission and secretary of health, education, and welfare. Ronald Reagan appointed him to be secretary of defense in 1981.

During his years at the Pentagon, Weinberger worked to protect the United States against the Soviet Union, which many people at the time perceived as the greatest threat to America. He became one of the most respected secretaries of defense in history and served longer than any previous secretary except for Robert McNamara (who served 1961–1968). Today, Weinberger is chairman of the influential *Forbes* magazine.